CHURCH FOLKS

BEING PRACTICAL STUDIES
IN CONGREGATIONAL LIFE

By

"IAN MACLAREN"

(DR. JOHN WATSON)

AUTHOR OF "BESIDE THE BONNIE BRIER BUSH,"
"THE MIND OF THE MASTER," "THE CURE OF SOULS," ETC.

NEW YORK
DOUBLEDAY, PAGE & CO.
1900

CONTENTS.

Church Folks.

I.

How to Make the Most of a Sermon.

Unto the success of a sermon two people contribute, and without their joint efforts the sermon must be a failure. One is the preacher and the other is the hearer, and if some art goes to the composition of the sermon, almost as much goes to its reception.

In the art of the hearer the first canon is practice, for it is a fact that the regular attendant not only hears more but also hears better than the person who drops into church once in two

months.   No doubt if the preacher has
lungs of brass, and the hearer is not
stone deaf, a casual can catch every
word on the rare occasion when he attends, although for the past six weeks
he has worshipped at home or made the
round of the neighboring churches.
There is some difference, however, between a steam whistle which commands
its audience within a given area without distinction, and a musical instrument to which ears must be attuned for
its appreciation.

The Chief Condition of Successful Hearing.

The voice of a competent speaker is
not so much sound merely, but is so
much music, with subtle intonations
and delicate modulations; his pronun-
ciation of a word is a commentary upon
it; his look as he speaks is a translation
of it; his severity is softened by the

pathos of his tone; his praise is doubled by its ring of satisfaction. A stranger's ear is not trained to such niceties; it is the habituated ear which reaps the full sense.

Besides, every speaker worth hearing creates his own atmosphere, and one cannot hear with comfort until he is acclimatized. The speaker has his own standpoint, and one must be there to think with him; he passes every word through his own mint, and one must be familiar with the stamping. Casuals are puzzled by the man, but his familiar friends are at home with him. ."He said this or that," the casual urges. "Oh, yes," answers the expert, "but with him that means something more." Perhaps the chief condition of successful hearing is to know the speaker, his working axioms, his special devotion, his unconscious prejudices, his characteristic message, and this knowledge can only be got by continual hearing.

WHEN A MINISTER REVEALS HIMSELF.

It is not in private that a minister really reveals himself; it is in the pulpit. When you met him on Saturday upon the street he spoke of the weather or about a book, hiding himself, as every real man does, in ordinary intercourse; on Sunday, without knowing, he drops his mask till you can read his character and have seen his soul. Of course, some men are as veiled in preaching as in conversation, but in that case their hearers have lost nothing; there is no individuality to reveal, only a lay figure beneath the conventional garments of the day. It takes one month of constant wear to break in a pair of heavy walking boots, and at least six months to fit into a new study chair; a year of constant attendance is required to place one on easy terms with a preacher, and then the advantage must not be thrown away.

Scottish Congregations Which Appear Asleep.

The second canon is attention, which comes to this, that a hearer shall make his body serve his soul in church. People may be listening when they sit motionless with their eyes shut, and many explain that they have simply withdrawn themselves from a disturbing environment, but in that case they ought to give some sign of life at intervals, if only to reassure the preacher and to save their neighbors from the sin of uncharitable judgment. There are congregations in Scotland where one-third of the audience appears to be asleep, but the preacher is afterward assured that these very hearers could give the best account of his sermon and are the keenest critics of his orthodoxy. They do not, however, form an exhilarating spectacle for the preacher, and his temptation will often be to say something heterodox in order to compel them to give some sign of interest.

If any one, on the other hand, is afflicted by the evil spirit of restlessness which is ever impelling him to fidget and sometimes drives him beneath the book-board, then this man ought either to master his tormentor by practice at home, or he should be placed in some special seat where he may hear but not be seen.

Audiences of Studied Negligence.

Nor does it, in any way, assist sympathetic hearing for a man to fold his arms and throw himself into his seat as one who knows what is before him and will endure to the end without flinching. A preacher may at any time refer to the noble army of martyrs, but he does not wish to address a body of martyrs in his own church. Nothing will more certainly discourage a preacher, till the words break on his lips and he can hardly maintain grammar, than an audience in every attitude of studied negligence, and nothing will more certainly inspire him than one unbroken expanse of intelligent faces.

When a Sermon Can be Heard Aright.

Next comes concentration, and here the trained hearer has an enormous advantage. If it be difficult for some people to listen, it is ten times harder for other people to follow, for it is evident a person may listen and not follow. Very few are accustomed to think about the same thing, or, indeed, to think about anything, for thirty minutes; after a brief space their interest flags and they fall behind; they have long ago lost the thread of the preacher's argument and have almost forgotten his subject. The sermon which suits such

a desultory mind is one of twenty para-
graphs, each paragraph an anecdote or
an illustration or a startling idea, so
that wherever the hearer joins in he can
be instantly at home. Sensible people
ought, however, to remember that a
series of amusing lantern-slides and a
work of severe art are not the same, and
if any one is to expound the gospel of
Christ worthily he must reason as he
goes and ask his hearers to think.   The
chain may be of gold, but there ought to
be links securely fastened together, and
a hearer should try them as they pass
through his hands. If one does not
brace himself for the effort of hearing
a sermon he will almost certainly finish
up by complaining either that the
preacher was dull or that the discourse
was disconnected.   No sermon is worth
hearing into which the preacher has not
put his whole strength, and no sermon
can be heard aright unless the hearer
gives his whole strength also.

What a Preacher is Entitled to.

My fourth canon of successful listening is candor, and a preacher is entitled to ask this quality of his hearer. If a juryman enters the box with his mind made up regarding the case, then it is vain for any counsel to speak, and there is no hope of securing a just verdict. If a person enters church with hopeless prejudices in the matter of truth, then it does not matter how able or how eloquent the preacher may be, he cannot get access to that hearer's mind. The honest hearer is one who is willing to consider every argument and to revise every conclusion, except, of course, those half dozen outstanding verities which no preacher of intellectual sanity would ever attack and which every religious person accepts as final. There are, however, many sides of truth which a hearer may never have seen and many applications of truth which

may never have occurred to him.
He ought to be willing to follow the
preacher as a guide and at least to judge
the prospect for himself: he ought to
be willing to consider how far the
preacher's word affects his own conduct.

Nothing stimulates a preacher and
gives him greater confidence in expounding truth than the assurance that
every word which he speaks from an
honest mind will be considered by
honest hearers. He feels that if they
agree with him, it will be because they
have been convinced; if they disagree
with him, it will be because in their
judgment he has failed to make good
his plea.

The Atmosphere Killing to a Church.

And the last canon is charity, which
blesses twice—the man who preaches

and the people who hear. No atmosphere is so injurious to the hearer, and none so trying to the preacher, as petty criticisms and malicious interpretation. People ought to hear in a large and generous spirit, remembering that the preacher is a man of like frailties with themselves, and remembering that no man ought to be judged except on the length and breadth of his teaching. It is possible that one day he may be dull —it is a matter of the weather; it is possible another day that he may not be sweet-tempered—it is a matter of digestion; the hearers ought to make great allowances for one who has to work with the double instrument of a fickle mind and an imperfect body. Hearers should lay it down as a rule that no man ever can be equal except he travel on the plane of dreary commonplace.

The Preacher Who is Always the Same.

It is said that once a deputation from a vacant congregation went to hear a middle-aged doctor of divinity, a man of placid disposition and uninspired mind. After hearing him preach a sermon which he had prepared on the Monday forenoon preceding, and the like of which he could have prepared every forenoon following, they asked one of his congregation whether that was a fair specimen of the doctor's preaching. "Ye may," he said, "depend on that; hear him once ye hear him ever; he's aye the same; there are no ups and downs with the doctor." Certainly he never descended below the even road of bare common sense, and certainly he never ascended to the heights of inspiration. Many preachers find that every fourth or fifth Sunday, as the case may be, they fail, beating

the ground with their wings, and not
being able to rise. Their congregations
will receive ample compensation on the
Sunday following, and they will enjoy
the top of the mountain, with its far
view and breezy atmosphere, all the
more on account of the valley wherein
they walked and were shut in.

The Cruelest Act of the Pew.

One of the cruelest acts of injustice
on the part of the pew is to suspect the
preacher of personality and to read
unthought-of meanings into his words.
Should a preacher describe with much
minuteness of detail and a certain
keenness of feeling any particular sin,
his hearers ought to be certain that he
is describing his own sin, for, indeed,
no man knows any sin as he knows his
own.

It is best for the hearer to believe
that the preacher is moved simply in
everything he says by loyalty to truth

and by the love of his fellow-men, and that no one regrets so bitterly as he does any shortcoming in exposition or any defect in the spirit of his teaching. His desire is to convince and to comfort; his one reward the spiritual help which he affords to the souls of his fellow-men. If by his words any brother man is strengthened to do his work with more faithfulness during the week, or is succored amid the trials of life, then he has not failed in his calling and does not regret his sacrifices. His endeavor is the highest known in human life and his labor is the hardest. Unto him therefore should be extended the utmost sympathy, and for him there should be offered the most constant and earnest prayer.

Listening Without Practice No Use.

No hearer has given a preacher a fair chance if he forgets what has been said at the church door, or if he treats a sermon as an essay to be discussed. The church is not a place of recreation nor a debating society: it is a school, where the chief lesson of knowledge is taught —how to live. The instructions are given from the pulpit; the demonstration must be made at home. Above all religions, Christianity is experimental and practical—a set not of rules, but of principles which must be wrought out in the details of each man's life. That preacher has understood his duty and done it who moves a man to action, and that hearer has made the utmost of a sermon who has proved it in practice. It is not necessary that the preacher be didactic, saying as to children, "You must do this or that," which is insufferable and ineffectual. The best preachers are suggestive, making men ashamed of low living by the exposure of sin, and moving men to nobility by exhibiting the beauty of

virtue.   The honest hearer does not do
good afterward because he was told, but
because he must.   He has opened his
heart to the message of truth as soft
spring soil for the seed, and in this
hospitable home the seed springs up.

THE CHIEF END OF EVERY SERMON.

Above   all   things,   the   Christian
preacher makes two demands, and both
can be justified only by the obedience
of the hearer.   He invites his audience
to become   disciples   and   servants   of
Jesus; he magnifies the Master's grace
and power; he assures his fellow-men
that to trust in Jesus and to follow Him
is to live.   If the hearer argues and
debates about Jesus, he can never arrive
at the facts, and he has not dealt fairly
with the preacher.   Let him put the
matter to the test and make the adven-
ture with Jesus as did the first Christians.   If he does, then he will be able
to judge the preacher; if not, he ought

to be silent. Never has there been more
futile criticism than that of hearers who
will not believe: such people wander
round the outside of the cathedral and
discuss the painted glass, which can
only be understood from the inside.
Another appeal of the Christian
preacher is for sacrifice, and it is his
duty to magnify the glory of unselfish
living. He asks people to do what is
hard and unattractive, and promises
them a gain which is spiritual and
unseen. It lies upon the hearer to
verify this commandment for himself,
and to find out whether serving others,
and not one's self, does make one hap-
pier and stronger.

The chief end of preaching is, after
all, inspiration, and the man who has
been set on fire is the vindication of the
pulpit. The chief disaster of preaching
is detachment and indifference. Never
was any sermon so poor and thin but it
contained more than its hearers could

practise.   No sermon has failed which
has sent one man away richer by a
single thought, or stirred to a single
brave deed.

II.

How to Make the Most of Your Minister.

Between a minister and his congregation there is an action and a reaction, so that the minister makes the congregation, and the congregation makes the minister. When one speaks of a minister's service to his people, one is not thinking of pew rents and offertories and statistics and crowds, nor of schools and guilds and classes and lectures. The master achievement of the minister is to form character and to make men. The chief question, therefore, to consider about a minister's work is: What kind of men has he made?

And one, at least, of the most decisive questions by which the members of a congregation can be judged is: What have they made of their minister? By that one does not mean what salary they may give him nor how agreeable they may be to him, but how far he has become a man and risen to his height in the atmosphere of his congregation. Some congregations have ruined ministers by harassing them till they lost heart and self-control, and became peevish and ill-tempered. Some congregations, again, have ruined ministers by so humoring and petting them that they could endure no contradiction, and became childish. That congregation has done its duty most effectively which has created an atmosphere so genial, and yet so bracing, that every good in its minister has been fostered and everything petty killed.

What the Congregation Must Do.

A young minister is a charge committed to a congregation, and its first duty is patience, especially with his preaching. One extremely young, and, what is not the same thing, very immature, minister began life as assistant in a city church famous for its activity and earnestness. His work was to visit sick people and to attend to details, and, wisely, he was seldom asked to preach. When he did preach his sermon was a very boyish performance indeed—shallow, rhetorical, unpractical—and he had sense enough to be ashamed. By and by he was appointed, for accidental and personal reasons, to a church of his own in a remote country district. Before he left the big city church, one of the elders called to bid him farewell. He said he felt that it was only right to point out where the assistant had succeeded and where he had failed.

" You have been very attentive to the invalids and—er—the children, and I may say without flattery that you have been well liked, but you know that God has not given you the power of public speech. I am afraid you will never be able to preach. Still, you may have much usefulness and blessing as a pastor."

It was not a cheering prospect to wait on old ladies and attend Sunday-school treats, but the lad thanked the candid elder with a sinking heart, and went to his new work.

What One Man Did for His Minister.

His first experiences in the new parish seemed to confirm the pessimistic prophecy. One day he forgot everything in the middle of his sermon; another day, in expounding an epistle of Saint Paul, he had got his thoughts

into such a tangled skein that he had
to begin again and repeat half his exposition.   On that occasion the young
minister was so utterly disheartened
that he formed a hasty resolution in the
pulpit to retire, and went into the
vestry in the lowest spirits.   There an
old Highland elder was awaiting him
to take him by the hand and to thank
him for " an eloquent discourse."

" It is wonderful," he said in his
soft, kindly accent, " that you are
preaching so well, and you so young,
and I am wanting to say that if you
ever forget a head of your discourse,
you are not to be putting yourself about.
You will just give out a Psalm and be
taking a rest, and maybe it will be
coming back to you. We all have plenty
of time, and we all will be liking you
very much.   The people are saying
what a good preacher you are going to
be soon, and they are already very
proud of you."

Next Sunday the minister entered
the pulpit with a confident heart, and
was sustained by the buoyant atmosphere of friendliness; and as a conse-
quence he did not hesitate nor forget,
nor has he required since that day to
begin again.   Little wonder that his
heart goes back from a city to that
Highland parish with affection and
gratitude; had it not been for the charity of his first people he would not now
be in the ministry.

A Congregation Must Stand by its Minister.

The members of a congregation are
bound to stand by their minister in the
outer world.   He is their own, and they
ought to be jealous of his good name.
If he says or does what is less than
right, let them tell him face to face in
all tenderness and love; but if strangers criticise him, let his people defend

and praise. If a man's own household is loyal, then he is not cast down by the hostility of the man on the street. When it turns against him he loses heart. Nothing will teach a proper man to judge himself more severely or to realize his faults more distinctly than the discovery that his critics in private are his advocates in public.

It happened once that a leading member of a congregation considered it his duty to remonstrate with his minister, to whom he was deeply attached, because the minister's preaching had grown hard and unspiritual. They were personal friends, and the conversation was conducted with perfect taste and temper; but the minister did feel a little sore afterwards, which was rather foolish, and he worried himself with the idea that his friends and his congregation were turning against him. A few days afterward a brother minister called upon him, and as they

talked of one thing and another his
visitor congratulated him on the attach-
ment of his people. " Why, last night
at a dinner-table old Doctor Sardine
was carping at your preaching—calling
you a rationalist, and so forth—when
Mr. Cochrane spoke out at once and
told the old gentleman that he did not
know what he was talking about. ' I go
to his church,' said your man, ' and I
know that I can never repay my minister all that he has done for me and
mine.' It was straight talk, and produced an immense impression, and one
minister envied you such a friend."

Nothing Helps a Minister Like Confidence.

While his friend had told him his
faults boldly, man to man, and he had
taken private offence, like a foolish
child, that friend had been guarding
his reputation with generous enthusi-

asm, and at the thought thereof he was moved to repentance. The judgment of his friend received a new weight, being sanctioned by such pledges of sincerity and magnanimity. So it came to pass in the end that the minister reconsidered his position and realized that he had fallen into extremes. Nothing has a more wholesome effect on a high-spirited man than the sense that a number of people trust him and guard him, and are ready to stand or fall with him. This confidence inspires him with humility, tones down his pride, teaches him caution, and lays on him the responsibility of carrying himself well in the conflict of life.

A wise congregation will also respond to the highest which the minister gives, and will discriminate between the second-rate and first-rate product of his brain. There is such a thing as a cheap sermon, which may be very popular and showy, with a shallow cleverness.

Bright men are often tempted to preach such sermons because they are easily thrown off, and do not strain the soul. And a congregation is apt to welcome such sermons because they demand little attention.

Congregations Must Listen with their Souls.

There is such a thing as a dear sermon, which has cost a man agony of brain and heart—a sermon charged with thought and passion. Such sermons are not lightly prepared nor can they be lightly heard. As the preacher has put his soul into his work, so the people must put their souls into the hearing. Of course, a strong man will not cease to put forth his hardest, choicest work, although no one approves, and he will not fall beneath his best in any circumstances; but the desire for cheap and popular preaching puts a heavy strain on the resolution of an ordinary minister until he is sometimes tempted to please the foolish people in his congregation, and to lighten his own burden by giving them less than his best. And it is the saddest of all ironies in church life when a man succeeds, as far as outside appearances go, who has buried his talents, and a congregation is happy and apparently satisfied which has wasted its minister.

If a minister be inspired by high ideals and has an iron will, he will fulfil himself in spite of the most debilitating circumstances, and although his people clamor for cheap cleverness, he will insist on feeding them with the finest of the wheat. Many worthy men, however, are neither particularly strong nor spiritual, and if their people have no appetite for strong meat, they will satisfy them with the poorest of all claptrap—the claptrap of religion. It may be evangelistic verbiage or social rant or rationalistic cant, but it is the by-product of the man's mind, and worse than worthless to the members of his church.

The Minister Must Lead His People.

The minister should be given to understand that his congregation expects to share in the ripest knowledge he possesses, and will appreciate his most careful thinking. When he rises to his height on any occasion and preaches a great sermon it does not matter whether every person has understood every word or some of them only about one-half. He ought to be told that all the members of his church are proud of him and thank God for him, and that even if he were beyond them, this was not because of obscurity, but because of elevation, and that they are pleased to have a minister who lives at

such a level. He must not come down
to them, but they must strive to rise to
him. It is a miserable business for
a preacher to repeat the commonplaces
of his people in a showy form so that
the man in the street goes home con-
gratulating himself because he has
heard his paltry ideas tricked out in
a showy dress. It is the function of the
prophet to lead his flock onward, even
though the march be sometimes through
the wilderness, and they ought to follow
close behind him and tell him that they
are there, and that they will not cease
to follow till he has brought them into
the fulness of the Land of Promise.
Under those conditions a man will feel
bound to read the best books and to
think out every subject to its very
heart; he will grudge no labor of brain,
no emotion of soul, to meet the expectation of a thoughtful, broad-minded
people, and if he come at last to be
a leader of thought whose words fly far

and wide, then to this congregation will
the credit be due who believed in him
and demanded great things of him and
made more of him than he, in his most
ambitious moment, could have imag-
ined.

Ministers Need Constant Encour-
agement.

It is also the duty of the members of
a congregation to encourage their minister, and they would take more trouble
to do so if they only knew how much
he needed their encouragement, and how
much he would thrive upon it.   They
must have a strong imagination in order
to understand the trials of his lot, which
are different from those of every other
worker, because he has to work by faith
and not by sight.   As he sits in his
study and at midday has not written
a line because his thoughts would not
flow, or when he burns four hours' work

because it is worthless, the minister
looks out and envies a workman who,
across the street, has completed in the
same time so many feet of brickwork
which is as good as it could be, and will
last for many a year. As he visits the
sick of his flock, anxiously looking for
some sign that his words of comfort and
advice have produced their due effect,
he wishes he were a physician, who can
see the good he does and has his quick
reward in lives saved from death—in
bodies relieved from pain. It sometimes seems to the minister as if his
words from week to week were wasted
—so much water poured on the desert.
From the very nature of the case he
cannot discover the fruit of his ministry, and therefore others should tell him
that he has not labored in vain. People
are quick enough to criticise a sermon
or to dwell upon the fact that the attendance has been a little scantier of late,
but is there nothing else they could

mention to the pastor? Has he never thrown light on some difficult passage of Scripture nor stimulated the conscience to the sense of some new duty nor sustained the heart in some sorrow of life? Why should he be left in ignorance who waits so wistfully for news which does not come and which would mean so much?

One Letter Which Inspired a Sermon.

Let me take you to the interior of a study where the minister is toiling with laboring oar and despairs of ever reaching land. The forenoon mail arrives and four letters are laid upon his table: one is uninteresting, one is tiresome, one is vexatious, and the disheartened man opens the fourth letter with a sigh. Another complaint from some querulous person; another detail laid on a weary man! What is this?

" My Dear Pastor: For some time I have
wished to write and tell you what a help you
have been to those who are very dear to me.
Again and again my husband has been cheered
and encouraged in his fight to do what is right
in business by your brave words. He told me
one Sunday night that nothing had done so
much to keep him straight as your sermons.
You know that Jack made us rather anxious
for some time because he seemed careless and
indifferent to home. Well, he has quite changed
of late, and is so attentive to me and nice with
his father. And on my birthday he brought
me such a lovely present, for which he must
have been saving during months. When I
told him how grateful I was he only said: ' It
was that sermon on sons and mothers did it.'
And now last Sunday your sermon on care
seemed to be written for me, for I have so little
faith and am so anxious. So I must tell you
that you have inspired the life of one household and that we bless God for you.

" Yours most gratefully,
" May Harrison."

It may not seem a long letter nor one
difficult to understand, but the minister
was not satisfied till he had read it six
times. And although it may not seem
a learned letter, it shed such a flood of
light on the text that the minister's pen

flew. He locked that letter up in his
desk, but found that he had forgotten
a sentence, so it was more convenient
to carry it in his pocket. On Sunday he
judged it necessary to read that letter
before going to church, and he had a
last peep at it in the vestry. And the
minister preached that morning with
such power and hope that even the
grumblers were satisfied, and the congregation went home on wings.

III.

THE CANDY-PULL SYSTEM IN THE CHURCH.

As I write, the appeal of a Young Men's Christian Association to its members lies on the table before me, and I copy it verbatim:

"DO NOT FORGET

The next Social
The next Candy-pull
The next Entertainment
The next Song Service
The next Gospel Meeting
The next Meeting of the Debating Club
The next Chicken-pie Dinner
The next date when you ought to make the secretary happy with your cash."

This remarkable list of operations, combining evangelistic zeal, creature

comforts, and business shrewdness, requires no commentary: the items give
us a convincing illustration of an up-
to-date religious institution—a veritable
hustler of a Y. M. C. A.

Perhaps one department of the work
requires a word of explanation; there
may be some persons who have given
considerable attention to Christian
agencies, and yet whose researches may
not have come across a " candy-pull."
This agency, if that be the correct word,
is a party of young men and women
who meet for the purpose of pulling
candy, and, in the case of the co-
operation of sexes, is said to be a very
engaging employment. It may be
that candy-pulling on the part of a
Y. M. C. A. is confined to one sex, and
is therefore shorn of half its attraction,
but one clings to the idea that in these
days of " pleasant" religious evenings
the young men would not be left to their
own company.

Conducting a Church on Modern Lines.

The Christian church and a Y. M. C. A. are, of course, very different institutions, and the latter is free from any traditions of austere dignity; but one is not surprised to find that the church has also been touched with the social spirit and is also doing her best to make religion entertaining. One enters what is called a place of worship and imagines that he is in a drawing-room. The floor has a thick carpet, there are rows of theatre chairs, a huge organ fills the eye, a large bouquet of flowers marks the minister's place; people come in with a jaunty air and salute one another cheerily; hardly one bends his head in prayer; there is a hum of gossip through the building.

A man disentangles himself from a conversation and bustles up to the platform without clerical robes of any kind, as likely as not in layman's dress. A quartette advances, and, facing the audience, sings an anthem to the congregation, which does not rise, and later they sing another anthem, also to the congregation. There is one prayer, and one reading from Holy Scripture, and a sermon which is brief and bright. Among other intimations the minister urges attendance at the Easter supper, when, as is mentioned in a paper in the pews, there will be oysters and meat— turkey, I think—and ice-cream. This meal is to be served in the " church parlor."

As Soon as the Benediction is Said.

No sooner has the benediction been pronounced, which has some original feature introduced, than the congregation hurries to the door; but although no one can explain how it is managed, the minister is already there shaking hands, introducing people, "getting off good things," and generally making things "hum." One person congratulates him on his "talk"—new name for a sermon—and another says it was "fine."

Efforts have been made in England also to make church life really popular, and, in one town known to the writer, with some success of its own kind. One church secured a new set of communion plate by the popular device of a dance; various congregations gave private theatricals, and one enterprising body had stage property of its own. Bible classes celebrated the conclusion of their session by a supper; on Good Fridays there were excursions into the country, accompanied by a military band, and a considerable portion of the congregational income was derived from social treats of various kinds. This particular town is only an illustration of the genial spirit spreading through-

out the church in England. One minister uses a magic lantern to give force
to his sermon; another has added a tav-
ern to his church equipment; a third
takes up the latest murder or scandal;
a fourth has a service of song; a fifth
depends on a gypsy or an ex-pugilist.

If this goes on, the church will soon
embrace a theatre and other attractions
which will draw young people and prevent old people from wearying in the
worship of God.

Is the New Departure an Improve-
ment?

Perhaps it may be the perversity of
human nature which is apt to cavil at
new things and hanker after the good
old times—which were not always good,
by any means—but one is not much
enamored with the new departure nor at
all convinced that what may be called
for brief the "Candy-pull" system is any

improvement on the past. After a slight experience of smart preachers and church parlors and ice-cream suppers and picnics, one remembers with new respect and keen appreciation the minister of former days, with his seemly dress, his dignified manner, his sense of responsibility, who came from the secret place of Divine fellowship, and spoke as one carrying the message of the Eternal. He may not have been so fussy in the aisles as his successor nor so clever at games nor able to make so fetching a speech on " Love, Courtship, and Marriage."

Was the Old-Time Clergyman too Formal ?

The members of his congregation may not have called him a " bright man" nor said he was " great fun" nor asked him so often to tea-parties, and it may be granted that he erred on the side of formality; but, on the other hand, they spoke of him as a " man of God" and a " good man," and in the straits of life and in anxiety of conscience they sent for him. They may not have liked him so well as the modern man, but they respected and trusted him, which is far more important.

One is also struck by the change in the whole environment of worship, and there may be a difference of opinion whether it has been for the better or the worse. The church of our fathers was not well lighted nor scientifically ventilated nor elaborately cushioned, and all there could be seen of carpet was on the pulpit stairs. The church of to-day is amazingly decorated, and bright with innumerable electric lights.

Congregations Meet to Listen to the Choir.

The service of the past was musically imperfect and was generally too long.

To-day the tenor in the choir is dismissed if his voice shows signs of wear,
and the people sit in judgment on how
the anthem has been "attacked" or
"rendered"—perhaps it was "Holy,
Holy, Holy, Lord God Almighty"—and
there is a notice in the vestry (or minister's parlor) that the Scripture lesson
must not exceed fifteen verses—ten is
preferred—and the prayers must not
encroach on the music, and the sermon,
whatever be its subject, even though it
be the Judgment Day, must be "interesting." In the former time a congregation used to speak of a sermon as
"edifying" or "searching" or "comforting." Now it declares that the
preacher was in "great form," or it
complains that he was "off color."

There are, no doubt, many points in
which the congregation of the present
has advanced on the congregation of the
past, but it has not been all gain, for
the chief note in the worship of the

former generation was reverence—
people met in the presence of the
Eternal, before whom every man is less
than nothing. And the chief note of
their children, who meet to listen to a
choir and a clever platform speaker, is
self-complacency.

Fear of God Seems to Have Departed.

It ought to be granted that one reason
for this change in the spirit of congregational life is a reaction from
individualism and a new conception of
the fellowship of the Christian church.
A religious person no longer thinks of
himself as a solitary unit, isolated from
every other human being in the world,
and whose chief business in life is to
save his own soul. He has realized that
his life is bound up with that of his
neighbors, and that he is a member of
a society which extends over all the

world; that he must not deny his humanity, and that in saving others he is also saving himself. The world is no longer a wilderness through which he marches a pilgrim and stranger, but his birthplace, to which he owes a duty, and religion is not so much an austere devotion to God as it is a useful, charitable life.

The centre of thought has, in fact, shifted from eternity to time, from the worship of God to the service of men. The one idea was enshrined in a Puritan meeting, where each man waited in wistful expectation for a sign of favor from the Almighty, or in the cathedral where the multitude bowed in silent adoration at the lifting of the Host. The other idea is visible in the building, more concert-room than church, where a number of good people meet in high spirits and in kindly fellowship to move one another to good works, and to sing hymns. The ancient fear of God seems

to have departed entirely, and with it
the sense of the unseen, which once
constituted the spirit of worship.

The Up-to-Date Church Needs an Annex.

Religion, it is urged with considerable force, must provide not only for
the soul, but also for the mind and body,
so that a Christian will not need to go
outside the church for culture or
amusement. If he want relaxation,
entertainments must be provided for
him at his church, so that he need not go
into worldly society; and whatever be
his intellectual taste, it must be met in
his ecclesiastical home. His literary
and debating society and drawing-room
and concert must be all under one roof,
so that the young Christian may be
sheltered from temptation.

As this social tendency of the congregation is becoming more marked every

year, and new inventions are being
added, it is vain to urge a return to the
simplicity of the past, when a congregation was a body of people who met
to worship God and study His will;
but it may be worth while to point to
certain drawbacks in the new develop-
ment. For one thing, if congregations
are to become " universal providers,"
another kind of minister will be needed.

How the Modern Minister Pre-
pares Himself.

For this kind of institution a teacher
to expound the Bible or a pastor to
train the character of his people is
hardly needed, and certainly he would
not be appreciated. The chief requisite
demanded is a sharp man, with the
gifts of an impresario, a commercial
traveller, and an auctioneer combined,
with the slightest flavor of a peripatetic
evangelist. Instead of a study lined

with books of grave divinity and classical literature, let him have an office with pigeon-holes for his programmes and endless correspondence; cupboards for huge books, with cuttings from newspapers and reports of other organizations; a telephone ever tingling, and a set of handbooks: "How to Make a Sermon in Thirty Minutes," or "One Thousand Racy Anecdotes from the Mission Field."

Here sits an alert, vivacious, inventive manager, with his female stenographer at a side table, turning over one huge book to discover who is next in order of time for visitation, and another for details of families, or hastily examining filed speeches of public men on some subject to be taken on Sunday. From morning to night he toils, telephoning, telegraphing, dictating, compiling, hurrying around, conducting " socials " or " bright evenings," giving " talks," holding receptions, an un-

wearied, adroit, persevering man. No
one can help admiring his versatility
and honesty of intention; but if he is
to be the type of the minister of the
future, then he will supersede and ex-
clude a better man.

Should the Pulpit be Given to Managers?

There are men who possess every
becoming gift of learning and insight
and devotion and charity who are absolutely incapable of " running" a church
on modern lines. They could guide
a soul in spiritual peril, but they have
no talent for amusing young people;
they can declare the Everlasting Gospel
of the Divine Sacrifice, but they have
no turn for machinery; they can expound the principles of righteousness,
but they refuse to meddle with a recent
strike of motormen.

As regards the gain of the new depart-

ure, is it certain that the socializing of
the Church will make her creed and life
attractive? If it come to be a competi-
tion between the amusements of the
Church (or her feasts) and the amusements of the world (and its feasts), is
there any sane person who thinks that
the Church can win ?   Like Cæsar, the
world offers her magnificent shows; the
Church, like Christ, presents the vic-
torious Cross.

The Church Must Not Leave Her High Place.

Why should the Church leave her
high place and come down into the
arena, where she will be put to shame?
Do men come to church for petty pleas-
ures fit only for children or for the
satisfaction of their souls and the con-
firmation of their faith? Would Christianity have begun to exist if the
Apostles had been " pleasing preachers"

and " bright men" and had given themselves to "socials" and "sales" and
"talks" ? The Church triumphed by
her faith, her holiness, her courage, and
by these high virtues she must stand in
this age also. She is the witness to
immortality, the spiritual home of
souls, the servant of the poor, the pro-
tector of the friendless; and if she sinks
into a place of second-rate entertainment, then it were better that her
history should close, for without her
spiritual visions and austere ideals the
Church is not worth preserving.

IV.

The Mutineer in the Church.

It takes all kinds of people to make a world, and it takes almost as many kinds to make a congregation, but it is not necessary for congregational completeness to possess a mutineer. By a mutineer one means a person we can easily identify, and at whose hands most congregations have sometimes suffered. He is not to be confounded with a Christian of old-fashioned opinions, who is occasionally disturbed by a sermon on " The Fatherhood of God," and will come to the minister's study to explain that he has always believed God to be a judge. This man is perfectly honest, and ought to be treated with all consideration, because he is simply loyal to his hereditary faith, and all the time would like to receive the new gospel. Let him have a warm corner in the room, and a comfortable seat, and free opportunity to run through as many texts as he wishes, and a candid hearing unto the hour of midnight. He is open to conviction, and even if he leave unconvinced, he will not go to set fire to the congregation. Not he; but he will explain everywhere that the minister is a faithful Bible student and a patient pastor, and that it is a privilege and a responsibility to sit in his church.

Do Not Confound Him with the Restless Person.

Nor must the word be applied to one of those restless people who are ever detecting some fault in affairs and who

weary every person with random sug-
gestions. One week he writes that a
woman was turned away from the
church prayer-meeting because the hall
was full—the minister is always
amused with this mythical person and
wishes he could see her in the flesh—
and he suggests that the weekday service should be held in the church. He
knows a hundred people who would be
willing to come—and this also pleases
the minister very much, because the
good man hardly ever attends himself.
Next week some mysterious person
informs this man that he has caught
cold through the draught from one of
the windows, and our friend writes
sixteen pages to advocate window curtains, which would make St. Peter's
itself hideous and worship impossible
for all self-respecting people. A month
later this same man is convinced that
the whole congregation is a rope of
sand, and ought to be bound up by a

general visitation on the part of the office bearers, for which he is good enough to sketch a plan; and every other week he will make a new suggestion in a voluminous letter, till his brethren are apt to say strong words about his meddlesomeness.

TREAT THE RESTLESS PERSON WITH RESPECT.

His brethren ought rather to possess their souls in patience and treat the worthy man kindly, for there is not a grain of mischief in him, nor is there a better-hearted man in the whole congregation. He will be quite pleased if he gets a civil answer, and I would suggest this form for such occasions:

"DEAR MR. JUMP: I have received your interesting letter and note your suggestion about the curtains. The matter is one which will require careful consideration, and I hasten to assure you that it is encouraging to the minister and workers of the church to find that the welfare of our church in every respect lies so near your heart. With very warm regard, believe me,

         " Yours faithfully,
         " JOB HOLDFAST, Pastor."

Mr. Jump will be quite satisfied with this letter, and in twenty-four hours will have forgotten that he ever proposed curtains. It will be worth while for a congregation to engage, say, one Jump, just to note defects and to keep things moving. Two Jumps might be too much for the congregation, and they had better dispose of the second.

THE OVER-SENSITIVE CHURCH MEMBER.

There is another person who ought not to be considered a mutineer, although he is very wrong-headed and may become a real nuisance. He is the man who is apt to be offended and to be " hurt," as he calls it, because some one passed him at the church door without speaking, or "said things" about him—he knows not what—behind his back, or objected to some plan which he proposed, or refused to do something he asked. Having worried his wife about the matter, and talked himself into a fever of wounded vanity, he gives everybody to understand that he has a grievance, and assumes the air of a martyr. As a formal protest he may even absent himself from church for two Sundays, and will be still further hurt if no one calls to inquire the reason. Of course, he is very provoking, but there is no malice in the man, and he ought to be gently treated. It is his misfortune rather than his fault that he has no scarf-skin and no protection against the inevitable friction of life. A gentle touch and a liberal use of spiritual ointment will cure his wounds —or, rather, scratches.

How to Detect the Genuine
Mutineer.

The mutineer is of another breed and
is an able-bodied miscreant, who will
strike a hard blow whenever he can get
an opportunity, and at any person
whom he can reach. His sole desire is
to do mischief, and the more pain he
gives the better is he pleased. He will
write insulting letters to the minister,
charging him with every sin from
heresy to lying. He will get up a public
controversy about the affairs of the congregation in any newspaper which is
foolish enough to insert his letters. He
will attack the most reasonable pro-
posals of the office bearers, and impute
to them the worst motives. He will move
through the congregation as an incen-
diary, and set fire to every inflammable
person. When he is in his glory he will
threaten proceedings in the church
courts or in the civil courts; and al-

though he will never carry them out, being a coward as well as a bully, he will take the preliminary steps, which cause talk and alarm. It will also be part of his rôle to pose as a straight-forward and honest man of unflinching rectitude and spiritual aims. What he does will always be under constraint of conscience, and he will summon himself and his opponents with much rhetorical effect before the bar of eternal justice. He is so big and blatant, and good people are so charitable and easily cowed, that they often take this man at his own value and come to terms with him.

He Should Receive Little Consideration.

As a matter of fact, he is an utter humbug from every point of view, and ought to receive no mercy. Neither his opinions nor his feelings nor his complaints nor his threatenings should receive one moment's consideration. His first challenge should be accepted as a declaration of war, and the war had better be without quarter; and it is astonishing how soon this brigand can be brought to his senses and to abject submission.

Should he be established in a congregation and have shown his hand, the wisest plan is to give him notice to quit. It is not usual to ask any member to leave a church, and very unusual if he happen to be a man of substance and position, as this fellow often is; but congregations are much too anxious to keep every person, and much too slow to recognize that some men's absence is more profitable than their presence. Their presence simply means turmoil and heartburnings, their absence peace and prosperity; their presence soon drives many quiet folk away; their absence would remove a stumbling-block.

His Influence is Always Detrimental.

Should he apply for admission to a church where his character is known, then he should be plainly refused. Why should any minister, if it depend on him, receive a man who has half-broken another minister's heart? Why should a congregation give house room to a man who has reduced the affairs of another to ruin? The chances are he has left like an army which has eaten up one country and now must go to devastate another. If there be any power in a congregation that can do it, let the door be slammed in this man's face, and as he wanders about churchless perhaps he may learn wisdom.

Should any one say that we are treating the mutineer unkindly and un-Christianly, then he is carried away by an excess of charity and is not facing the facts. To deal kindly with a muti-

neer is to be cruel to the minister and
the congregation.   Although he be only
a single individual, there is no end to
the mischief which this man can do.
For one thing, he will gravely affect
the preacher, and that in ways which
the congregation can hardly imagine.
No preacher who is worth the name
writes his sermons without reference
to his congregation, as if he were living in another planet and were dealing
only with the ideas of the study.   As
he sits at the table he is really in the
pulpit and the congregation in the
pews; he speaks to them, and they respond; he sees one head lifted and
another cast down, one rebuked and
another comforted, till the books of the
study disappear and the room is full of
human feeling. It is in this atmosphere
that the preacher will do his best work
and most perfectly fulfil his mission.
Suppose, therefore, that at the end of
a pew—and that is where he is certain

to be, in some prominent place—this rebel is sitting, pugnacious, insolent, and defiant: is he not apt to be an influence in the sermon?

EFFECT OF HIS PRESENCE IN THE CHURCH.

No doubt there are men with such mental self-control and superb indifference to circumstances that they will ignore his existence. These are men of the great order, and one cannot expect many in the ministry or in any profession. For them there are no rules, and for them no hindrances; they are invulnerable and irresistible. Upon ordinary men the mutineer has an irritating and deflecting power, so that a preacher, consciously or unconsciously, is ever taking him into account, and the sermon's course is to a certain extent regulated by this man's existence. If the minister be a gentle and fearful

man, he is apt to be over-considerate,
and will omit things which he ought
to have said lest he should give offence.
Instead of the sermon's pursuing its
straight way and reaching its destina-
tion with as little loss of distance as
possible, it will be timid and subdued
in style.   The preacher will be continually qualifying in order not to be caught
by this critic, or he will be continually
deferring lest he should give offence to
this mighty man.   People will have
a vague sense of weakness, but they may
never guess the cause.

THE PREACHER'S WAY OF DEALING
WITH HIM.

Suppose, however, the preacher be
a strong and determined man, but not
one of the larger minds and the broader
vision, then the mutineer will affect
him after another fashion.   From the
beginning of the sermon the preacher

will set himself to deal with this man
and to bring him to his senses. His
character and his actions will be de-
scribed and denounced and satirized
and threatened. He will be pelted with
the judgments of Holy Scripture; its
commandments will be laid to his back
like a lash; the invitations of the Gospel
will be denied him, and the historical
rascals of the Bible will be suggested
as his photograph. Unto any one who
understands the allusion it will seem
that this man is being hardly dealt
with; but to any one who thinks a little
deeper it will be seen that the preacher
is the victim. The preacher has grown
sour and vindictive; the sermon has lost
its grace and tenderness; and I know
not which is the greater calamity: a
preacher without magnanimity or a sermon without nobility.

HE IS A DISTURBING FACTOR EVERY-
WHERE.

Remove this man from his place in
that church and the minister will give
himself without disturbance to deal
both with saints and sinners in the love
of God.

The mutineer will also distinguish
himself in arresting the activity of the
church both in work and giving. Should
he have a place, say, in the Sunday-
school, he will quarrel with the superin-
tendent and every one of the teachers
in turn till he has the school to himself,
and then he will lament the decay of
Christian sacrifice in the spirit. If
he be appointed treasurer of a fund
under the idea that this will give him
something to do, he will be such an
offence that no one will subscribe; and
if he be not treasurer, he will declare
everywhere that the fund does more
mischief than good, and that those

desiring the welfare of the church should not subscribe.

And besides all these mischievous achievements, he will poison the life of the church so that, instead of being gracious and harmonious, it will become bitter and quarrelsome. If there be a dispute in the church, this man will foment it; and if it be possible to set two people by the ears, he will do it. When there is an honest difference of opinion he will see that it be turned into a feud; and if a new proposal be put before the people, he will get up an acrimonious debate.

EFFECTUAL METHODS OF TREATING HIM.

Perhaps the most effectual system with such a man is not scolding and storming, but a policy of isolation. As nature makes a cyst and encloses any strange material so that it be kept separate from the body, let this man be imprisoned in a place by himself. If he should offer any remark upon church affairs, let the other person answer on the state of the weather; and if he criticise a sermon, say that he is sorry to hear of his dyspepsia. If he rise to speak at a church meeting, let the silence be such as may be felt, and after he has spoken let the chairman call for the next business as if he had never existed. If he has ever to be spoken to, the best plan is to treat him as an absurdity, and play around him with ridicule, for this will give much innocent amusement to other people, and it is the particular attack which he cannot stand. Between loneliness and laughter he will depart to another church, and then let the happy congregation sing the Te Deum.

V.

SHOULD THE OLD CLERGYMAN BE SHOT?

ONE day, and perhaps quite suddenly, a congregation awakens to the fact that a certain calamity has befallen the minister which will cripple his power more and more every day and may also ruin the life of the congregation. It has nothing to do with his character, for he is really a much holier man, and perhaps also a much wiser one, than he was twenty years before, and certainly he commits fewer mistakes in word and deed than in the days of his youth. Nor does it concern his pastoral work—for he is more than ever the counsellor and friend of the people, speaking to them from a richer experience of life and a larger charity. It is not right to say that it touches his preaching, for that is likely to be quite as solid and as useful as it ever was. Indeed, he is saying the very things he used to say with much acceptance, and in the way he used to say them—long ago.

Nothing is wrong with him, only that he does not walk so quickly as he used to, that he speaks a little more slowly, and that last week he had to get older spectacles, that he does not always hear what is said to him, that his hair is passing from gray to white, that he is fatigued when going up a hill. It has happened to him just as it happens to other men: the minister is getting old.

OLD MINISTERS IMPERVIOUS TO NEW IDEAS.

As soon as they realize the fact—and it may be years before they do notice it—the heads of a congregation begin to grow uneasy. Age has its advantages in the office of the ministry, but it has also very evident disadvantages, and when the balance is struck perhaps a congregation is right in the idea that it is losing, and not gaining, under the ministry of an old man. For one thing —and it is a very serious one—a minister after a certain age is almost impervious to new ideas. Of course, the exact age will vary with different men, and it is dangerous even to hint at it, since the reader would always be able to mention exceptions. There are men to whose minds no new idea can find access at the age of thirty—men of hopeless dulness, who will be an incubus on a congregation all their days; and there are men whose minds will be hospitable to the latest ideas at the age of fourscore—men of unique mental freshness and vivacity.

With the average man there comes

a time when his mind crystallizes and his beliefs become absolutely fixed. He may not resent the discoveries of younger men; he certainly will not assimilate them. He may not oppose new methods of action; he certainly will not adopt them. His preaching may be absolutely as good as it was before, because it will be the same, without any addition of new thought; but it may be bad, comparatively speaking, because it should have much new material and should also be in much closer touch with the age.

He Comes to be a Brake Upon the Coach.

With middle age there is apt to set in a suspicion of the rising generation and a keen resentment of its standpoint, so that the middle-aged man falls into a critical and pessimistic mood. He comes to be a brake upon the coach, and while the brake is a useful thing in its own place, it is a poor substitute for horses.

If his work be in a city church, it is a grave question whether any minister can now discharge it with efficiency who is above sixty years of age. The multitude of details in a city parish, the excitement of the life, the severe demand upon the mind, and the heavy burden of responsibility call for a man in the prime of life, with an alert intellect and an unfailing body. It is likely as time goes on that men after, say, twenty years in a city will have to retire and take some quieter sphere in the country. They will be put, as it were, upon the semi-retired list.

Besides, as one cannot fail to notice, the average man of middle age in bidding good-by finally to youth himself also largely isolates himself from young people. They may be respectful to him, and he may be interested in them, but there is now no common language and no common sympathy. They are apt to think him an " old fogy" (and as a middle-aged man myself I am inclined to think we do grow old-fogyish), and he is apt to think them frivolous. There are few men who can bridge the gulf between two generations and be equally acceptable both to the young and to the old, and the difficulty will increase rather than diminish. And all this is the penalty of growing old or even passing middle age.

One Eminent Clergyman Suggested Shooting.

What, then, is to be done with this unfortunate man ? And the difficulty has been felt so acutely that a distinguished divine of our day—who is now dead—proposed that a minister who was past his prime should be taken out

(I presume to some sheltered spot)
and shot. His idea was that clerical
incumbents should be treated after the
same fashion as worn-out horses. It
has always been dangerous to use irony
in England since the days of Swift, for
although the English people may have
every other quality under the sun, they
certainly have not a quick sense of
humor, and I am not certain that some
people did not think that this eminent
person was serious in his savage suggestion. Certainly he expressed the
mind of some ungrateful and miserable
congregations, who would be immensely
relieved to get rid of an old servant in
the quickest and cheapest fashion.
Perhaps, also, it would be the kindest
thing to the minister when he discovers
himself to be an incumbrance on those
whom he loves and who once loved him,
to give him by some means the *coup de
grâce;* but there are objections on the
part of an interfering law to this sum-

mary method of disposal, and one must
abandon the idea of an ecclesiastical
knacker's yard.

If He Had Any Sense of Propriety He Would Die.

You have, then, four courses of action with this unfortunate man, who, if
he had had any sense of propriety would
have died decently of a short and
pathetic illness at the age of fifty-five,
and the first is that the congregation do
nothing and he be allowed to live out
his days in the pulpit. Very likely he
used to say about the age of thirty that
he would never continue in the ministry
after his leaf had become yellow; that
he wondered how old men could not see
that their day was past, and that it
would be better for them to be pottering
about in a country garden. When he
said these brave things he was standing
on the other side of the hedge, and now,

when he is double the age, he has quite
another view of the situation. He
declares that he never felt younger in
his life and never more fit to preach.
At times he grows heroic, and declares
that as long as he can crawl he will
mount the pulpit stairs and that he will
die in harness.

Foolish people (mostly old ladies)
will tell him that he never preached so
ably as he did last Sunday, and he will
incline his ear to this little circle of
admirers and will refuse the advice of
sensible men who have his welfare at
heart and who suggest to him that he
should of his own accord resign the
office he has so honorably filled. So it
will come to pass that church and city
will see one of the saddest tragedies:
a man scattering the congregation he
once gathered and flinging away the
reputation he once won.

To Suggest a Colleague Does Not Please.

Or the congregation may pluck up courage and insist upon the worthy old gentleman having a colleague. " We do not want to lose your services," it is explained to the minister by some shrewd diplomat who knows that the minister, not to speak of the minister's wife, is watching him all the time with suspicious eyes. " We only wish to relieve you of the heavy end of your work. Would it not be a good thing that we should secure a vigorous young man who would take care of the classes and all the details of the church work, and preach once a day to save you fatigue and allow you to go for a lengthened holiday from time to time ? You have been very good in not asking relief from preaching, but the congregation feels that it is only a bare duty to give you permanent assistance. Besides," and now the ambassador feels that the minister's wife is regarding him with contempt as a detected cheat and an utter humbug, " it would be a good thing for a young man to have the benefit of your preaching and advice."

Very likely the old gentleman, after a conference with his wife and her lady friends, will refuse to have anything to do with a colleague, and will explain that he will propose such a measure himself as soon as he really finds it necessary, and meantime that nothing could be worse for a young man than to be going about doing nothing. He will perhaps add, and add it with deep regret, that he is assured by influential members of the congregation that the intrusion of a colleague would undo all the work that has been done and rend the church in twain.

Trouble When He Consents to Have a Colleague.

Should, however, the minister agree to a colleague, the result in nine cases out of ten will be disastrous. Either the old man will so dominate his younger brother that the latter will have no room for his individuality and will never rise to his height, or the young man will set himself against the old, and with the younger people at his back will drive the senior minister from the church. It is indeed an unreasonable and unnatural position that two men should have equal authority, and all the more so when they are both so dependent on popular opinion. Was it ever heard of that there should be two captains in one ship, two commanders-in-chief in one army, or even two engineers working one engine? And yet sane people will propose, not that a minister should have assistants or

curates, but that he should have a colleague to share with him equal authority and equal responsibility.

FORCING THE OLD MINISTER TO RETIRE.

Of course, a congregation may make
it so uncomfortable for the man who
has served it during the best years of
his life that he will have no alternative,
and will be glad to leave, even if he go
to obscurity and poverty. And when
a congregation takes this way of cutting
the knot one almost despairs of Christianity. The meanest merchant who
ever wrangled over a cent would not
treat an old clerk as a body of Christian
people will sometimes treat a poor and
worn-out minister. They have used up
his youth and his manhood and his
enthusiasm and his energy; they have
had the bloom of his mind and the
harvest of his soul. For them he lived

and thought; for them in the days of his strength he exhausted himself every Sunday, and has permanently worn out his reserves of life. All that they could get out of him they have got, and now, after watching for a year or two, they have come to the conclusion that his best days are done, and they make him a trumpery presentation and bid him go. Then they go, cap in hand, to some popular young minister and entreat his favor, declaring that their hearts have gone out to him, and they believe it to be God's will that he should be their minister. And he, in his turn, comes, and soon is to be heard declaring that there never was such a loyal people. Let him wait a little while.

WHY NOT ORGANIZE A RETIREMENT SCHEME?

Would it not be better that each denomination should organize a retire-

ment scheme upon a large scale with
two conditions? The first would be
that every minister should be removed
from active work at the age of, say,
sixty-five, and afterward he might give
assistance to his brethren or live· in
quietness, as he pleases. The second
condition would be that he receive a
retiring allowance of not less than half
his salary up to, say, $4000. Should
any one say that such a law is arbitrary,
then the answer is that surely any
minister would prefer to retire by law
rather than by force, and that he would
be in good company, for he would share
the lot of every naval and military
officer and every civil servant and every
officer of any great corporation through-
out the civilized world.

And the Church must not fall behind
the State. Upon the personnel of her
ministry must she depend for her visible success, and her aim ought to be that
each congregation have a minister in

full strength of mind and body, and that each man, after he has exhausted himself in the service of the Church, should be kept in comfort during the remaining years of his life.

Aged Ministers in Active Duty are a Hindrance.

Short of immorality and unbelief, one cannot imagine a greater hindrance to the energy of the Church than a large proportion of aged and infirm ministers in active duty. For this will mean obsolete theology, the neglect of the young, isolation from the spirit of the day, and endless wrangling. Nothing would more certainly reinforce the energy of the Church than the compulsory retirement upon satisfactory terms of every minister above the age of sixty-five. For this would mean not only a reserve of good men upon whom the Church could depend in emergencies, but a perpetual tide of fresh thought.

At present, congregations have a grievance against old ministers who think they are young, and old ministers have a grievance against congregations who do not respect age, and between the two arise many scandals and breaches of the peace. When the Church is as well managed as a first-rate business concern, then this standing feud will be healed, and no one will be so much respected and loved in the Christian Church as the faithful minister who has served her in the fulness of his strength, and now in the days of his well-earned rest enriches her with his counsel.

VI.

THE MINISTER AND THE ORGAN.

SONGS of praise are a part of public worship with every body of Christians —except the Society of Friends, whom I sometimes regard with envy—and I wish it to be understood at once that I am not prepared to suggest their abolition. The saints of the Old Testament had a musical service which was enough to fill the heart of a ritualist with despair, and one can only faintly imagine the kind of life which the priest lived who was responsible for the Temple orchestra and had to deal with the players on instruments. The New Testament saints began without an orchestra, and really seemed to have managed

their praise for some time on common-
sense principles, doing the best they
could with joyful lips and singing
bravely in black prisons. But, like
many other good people, they did not
know when they were well off, and by
and by they invented the melancholy
chants which have been a drawback
to Christians of all generations.

One sometimes wonders how the
Friends are able to look so peaceful and
why their worship is so delightful, and
I am tempted to think it is because they
have no music in their service. Had we
none, a frequent cause of trouble would
be removed from many a congregation,
and the minister would hardly know
what to do with his time. Yet I wish
it to be distinctly understood at the
same time that I regard music as a
necessary part of divine worship, that
organists are the strength of the Christian Church, and that every person who
does not appreciate to the full his choir-

master and his choir is an ignorant and
ill-natured Philistine.

Why Consideration is Shown the Organist.

If there ever is any trouble in the
congregation about the music, and if
the minister ever worries himself, let it
be admitted at once that the congregation and the minister are alone to blame.
But there are difficulties, and they may
be mentioned in a spirit of becoming
humility. For one thing, the organist
is an artist, and every artist has a
nature of special refinement which cannot bear the rough-and-tumble ordinary
methods of life. With a man of common clay you deal in a practical,
straightforward, and even brutal fashion, arguing with him, complaining to
him, and putting him right when he is
wrong. But no man must handle
precious porcelain in such fashion, or

the artist will be instantly wounded
and will resign and carry his pathetic
story to every quarter, for he is lifted
above criticism and public opinion. It
is impossible to teach him anything;
it is an insult to suppose that anything
could be better; it is best to accept
what he gives, and to recognize that it
is his sphere to do as he pleases and the
sphere of every other person to declare
that what he does is, on every occasion,
too lovely for human words, and that
its effect is almost too much for exhausted human nature. This is the
tribute which the congregation ought to
pay to the most spiritual of artists, the
organist.

Music is What the Congregation Wants.

One really becomes impatient with
the minister, who ought to know better
and yet forgets his own place, owing to

a want of artistic appreciation and to an overweening sense of his own office. He encroaches on the organist and is justly punished. The minister ought to remember—and the congregation may assist him in remembering—that his work is subordinate to that of the artist, and that the rest of the service is simply intended to be a support and environment for the music. What the congregation wants to hear is, not his sermon, although I have never known an organist object to the sermon, provided the preacher did not occupy too much time. Indeed, many organists, I have reason to believe, welcome the sermon as a rest for their overstrung nerves. What the congregation really desires to hear is the anthem, and the success of the day depends upon its performance. When a minister has laid this fact to heart, and taken care that the people who have been raised into a Heaven which cannot be de-scribed by the singing are not unduly harassed by his stupid words, he has at least escaped one rock of offence.

It is also most provoking that a minister will interfere with a selection of hymns, and still harping on his sermon, will select hymns which correspond with its theme. Very likely the hymns may suit the text perfectly and may be very popular with the people, but it is only the organist who knows whether the tunes in the hymn-book be high or low class music. The tunes may be so popular that every person is thirsting to sing them with all his heart and at the pitch of his voice, but an organist will be simply aghast at the thought of a thousand people going at large, as it were, in his province. It is a privilege, and a doubtful one at the best, that they should be allowed to sing at all, but if it be granted, they must mingle trembling with their joy.

ORGANISTS ARE DOING AWAY WITH
POPULAR TUNES.

One of the chief efforts of a really
cultured organist—there are exceptions
—is to extirpate popular tunes and to
replace them with arrangements which
will teach the congregation to keep
silence. A case came to my notice at
one time—and when I hear of such
things I do not know how my brethren
have been made—where a minister
got into a white heat with an organist
because that eminent person had invented a tune of his own for " Rock
of Ages," which was a dream of
beauty and reduced the congregation
to distant admiration. Nothing is more
irritating to the musical temperament
than to hear the people, who are always
inspired with an insane desire to make
a joyful noise, get hold of a really fine
tune and make it afterward hateful to
delicate ears. Nothing is more neces-

sary than to guard the congregational praise from these follies and at once to remove from use even the noblest tune if the people have finally taken possession of it.

Only ceaseless vigilance on the part of the organist can secure the music from the incursion of the congregation, for they are so determined and full of mad ambition that they will even set themselves to master strange tunes, and in the course of a month will drown the choir with music which was intended to be beyond their reach; and the wrongheadedness with which a minister will support the congregation in this raid upon another man's kingdom deserves all the trouble which falls upon his head.

People Readily Subscribe to an Organ Fund.

There were days—and some of us who are no longer young can remember them—when no instrument was used in public worship, and when every aid of this description, except a tuning-fork, was judged to be a return to the elements of the Old Testament. But those were days of darkness. To-day we are living in a brighter age. A congregation may nowadays give so little to its minister that his wife hardly knows how to get respectable clothing for the family, and may not contribute anything worth mentioning to foreign missions and hospitals; but there is no self-respecting congregation which will not now insist on possessing an organ. People who will harden their hearts against the most useful charity will subscribe to an organ fund, and what cannot be secured by subscription will be obtained by a bazaar with gambling. When the organ is opened by a distinguished musician, who is brought from a distance, the congregation will regard him with awe as an almost supernatural

being, and will count the event of more
importance than a revival of religion.
They will be utterly overcome by the
extent and variety of sound which he
will bring from the instrument, and
when he uses the *Vox Humana* mothers
of families can only look at one another
and shake their heads as if they were
hearing sounds from the other world.
When he subtly suggests thunder by
turning on the full force of the organ,
the heads of the congregation will congratulate themselves by signal, because
every one can now see that they have
received full value for their money.

ECCENTRICITIES AND DEMANDS OF A
NEW ORGAN.

After the recital is over the great
man will improvise for his own amusement, and when it is possible for ordinary beings to speak to him, a little
group of deferential office bearers will

ask him what he thinks of the organ.
He may give a patronizing and guarded
approval, but he will be careful to point
out the number of stops which ought to
be added and the number of improvements in action which are absolutely
necessary. He will, in fact, suggest
that they have only got the mere foun-
dation of an organ, and that the com-
pletion will take many a year and be an
endless opportunity for spending. Perhaps he may be good enough to say that
some $1500, laid out in one or two
improvements he rapidly sketches, will
make the instrument respectable for an
ordinary organist; but he may leave
them under the impression that in order
to make it suitable for a master like
himself the congregation would require
to concentrate its financial resources
upon the organ for the next ten years.

If the congregation has been at all
lifted by the possession of its new
organ, nothing will so chasten vanity

and self-conceit as the visit of a musician who has taken a degree and has several letters after his name; and if any person depreciates his advice as that of a hypercritical player, and supposes there will be no further trouble about that organ, his innocence is delightful, and shows that he has never had anything to do with musical instruments in places of public worship.

Whatever trials the congregation may have had before with draughts in the building or questions of heating or difficulties in finance or disturbances with mutineers, all these things will be less than nothing compared with the eccentricities and demands of its new organ. If it be blown by hand, then it will be found so large that two blowers are required, and so it will be proposed to have a hydraulic engine. This engine will not go two Sundays out of four because the pressure of water has failed, and then some members of the congrega-

tion will have to work the bellows—if
these have been wisely left for convenience—and before they have finished
their work deacons of a stout habit of
body and unaccustomed to manual labor
will have quite a new feeling about that
organ and will confine their compliments to the Hebrew language.

When Real Tribulation Begins.

By and by it will be suggested that
the organ should be played by electricity; and the congregation, but especially
the minister and the authorities in
charge of the music, will now begin to
know what real tribulation means. The
readjustment, it is said, will take six
weeks, and be of a comparatively slight
character; it will really take about a
year, with some months thrown in, and
during that time the congregation will
have an opportunity of inspecting the
different parts of its organ in the

church hall and classrooms and passages and outhouses, where it will be lying in mysterious fragments.

During the interim the members of the congregation will have forgotten that it is impossible for educated people to praise God without instrumental music, and in sheer absence of mind they will be singing more heartily than they have done for the last ten years. As there is no organ, the fancy tunes will have to be given up, and the people will be allowed to worship God with all their might. Ignorant strangers coming into the church, and not remembering that there is no organ, will say they never heard better singing in their lives, and the choir will be insulted with compliments about the way in which they are leading the congregation, while there is really no high-class choir, one or two excepted, which does not consider it an impertinence that the congregation should dare to follow it, and

which does not want to go its own way
alone.

WILL BE SIX MONTHS IN THE DOCTOR'S HANDS.

When the organ is finally reformed
and the day comes for its reopening,
the congregation pretends to be delighted, but it has a shrewd idea that
the days of its liberty are over. The
members of the congregation may have
ventured to follow afar off an organ
driven by a water-engine with a choir
in correspondence, but they will not
have the audacity to intrude upon an
organ played by electricity and assisted
by a still more elevated choir. If the
congregation,   however,   be   willing,
through a sense of politeness, to keep
silent, the electric organ will have no
such scruples, for its extravagances will
be endless. If it consent to play the
first voluntary, it will finish up with a

long, melodious howl, for which no one
can hold the organist responsible, and
it will give melodious toots during the
prayers which may be responses, but
have not been arranged for; and then
in the middle of the Te Deum, through
some fit of pure cantankerousness, it
will take refuge in a stubborn silence.
For six months after the opening
it will be in the doctor's hands, and
for a year following will not have com-
pletely shaken off the habit of a gay
and frivolous youth, and the congregation will be torn between two minds—
secret satisfaction when the organ is not
going and it has a chance of singing
free, and a fierce desire to cart it away
and have it thrown into the nearest
river.

What between building and renewing
the organ and adding stops to the
organ and tuning the organ, the organ
will cost every year in interest on
capital and current expenditure enough

money to have kept a missionary in
foreign parts or to have supported a
minister in a poor district of the city;
and what it costs in anxiety to the
organist, who is apt to be blamed for
everything, and who has generally to
spend an hour in its recesses with his
coat off before service, and to the congregation in chronic irritation, would,
if reduced to money value and multi-
plied by the number of organ-ridden
churches, clear the debt off every foreign mission in the Anglo-Saxon world.

Choirs are Often Accused of Quarrelling.

My own experience of a choir and
also of an organist has been altogether
delightful, which is one of my singular
mercies of which I am not worthy; but
I move about in the world, and I have
heard things. As a choir consists, it is
presumed, of a number of select persons,

male and female, who have correct ears
and rich voices and are lovers of the
most delicate and spiritual of the arts
—the most refined persons, in fact, in
a congregation—one would take for
granted that the whole atmosphere of
a choir would be full of gentleness and
peace. Rumors, however, reach one's
ears that the power of quarrelling
within certain church choirs can only
be exceeded by the high spirit of a body
of Irish patriots, and that there is
almost nothing so trivial and invisible
but that it will set a choir by the ears.
It may be the place in the stalls or the
singing of a particular part or a correc-
tion of the choir-master or a word of
approval to another chorister or a remark dropped by one of the choir—so
tender are the feelings of a chorister—
anything or, for that matter, nothing,
will hurt. He will sulk or make un-
pleasant remarks or resign or drive
some other persons out, and then on

some great occasion all the members of the choir will resign and take themselves so seriously that the event will be considered equal in interest to a war. Upon the whole, the choir rather enjoys a crisis of this kind, for it gives stimulus to the artistic temperament. But there are some who do not enter wholly into the enjoyment. One of these is the wretched minister, who finds himself some Sunday in the position of being his own precentor, and who has to be the mediator in every dispute; and the others are the members of the congregation, who are apt to be set on fire by sparks from this musical conflagration, and who are never perfectly certain whether they may not some Sunday have to do their own singing.

When the Old Tunes Were in Vogue.

Times there are, but possibly they are foolish moments, when one remembers with fond and wistful regret a country kirk where a precentor raised that time-honored old Scots tune " Martyr-dom" with a powerful note, and a con-gregation of clear-voiced and big-lunged men and women took up the tune, none keeping silence, and sang the air glori-ously, with here and there a bass and a tenor, even, perhaps, an alto thrown in to enrich the music. And there are other times when one who ought to have known better things has been much stirred in his heart by hearing the people sing at a mission service one of those tunes which may not be very good music, and may lend themselves to loudness of voice, but which are well called revival tunes because they quicken the people's souls and give expression to their joy as for the first time they realize that God has loved them and has given for their salvation His only and well-beloved Son.

It is well that the praise of God

should have every assistance of good
taste and musical art in subordination
to the rights of the people, but it is best
that men should sing with lips which
God has opened and from hearts which
have been redeemed at Calvary.

VII.

The Pew and the Man In It.

VARIOUS changes have been wrought
in the interior of the church since the
days of our fathers, but no change is
more significant than the opening of
the pew, which in its way has been
almost as great a change as the lowering
of the franchise in England and the
abolition of political disabilities. One's
memory recalls the good old days,
which we call good largely because they
were old and are now hidden in a mist
of reverent affection. One sees the long
row of family pews, each carefully
secluded from its neighbor and shut in

from the common street of the aisle by
a door which was fastened inside by
a robust hasp or, in the case of superior
pews, by a little brass bolt.

WHEN THE PEW-OWNER WAS OF IMPORTANCE.

If the tenant of the pew belonged
to the upper circle of the district, he
covered it with cloth—red or green—
furnished it with a cushion three inches
deep—which contained in its recesses
the dust of twenty-five years—and a box
for Bibles with a lock, where the books
of worship could be kept in security
from a stranger's hand.   There were
also hassocks of a substantial character,
not for purposes of kneeling—for no
one in such a pew would have thought
of such an inconvenient effort—but that
people might have their feet comfortably propped.   And there were even
such delicacies of comfort as an elbow

rest in the pew, so that one fortunate
sitter might be able to hold up his head
with his hand as he listened to the
sermon.

It was an interesting sight, and one
cherishes it in grateful remembrance,
when the local dignitary came in on
Sunday morning to take possession of
his mansion and to share in divine
worship. The pew-opener, a shrewd
old man brought up in the atmosphere of kirks, and whose very face
suggested the most abstruse doctrines,
who had been speaking on professional subjects with the deacons of the
place, and had allowed fifty of the
commonalty to pass without more than
a faint nod and a reference to the
weather—couched in subdued tones—
comes forward to receive the chiefs of
the synagogue and to lead them to their
seats. He goes first down the aisle with
stately tread, looking neither to the
right hand nor to the left, followed by

Dives's wife; after her the children;
following them the stranger that was
within their gates, and, last of all, con-
tented and superior, Dives himself.

The Pew Door was Fastened with a Hasp.

On arrival at the mansion-house door
the pew-opener, dexterously unlocking
the door with one hand and wheeling
round on one foot, faces the procession
behind the open door as it stretches
half way across the aisle and stands
there after a little bow, looking straight
before him, deferential, yet not unconscious of his place in the hierarchy of
the church, and the members of the
family file in and take their places till
at last there is hardly room for the
great man himself. It will be enough,
however, if he can just sit down, for
in that case the influence of a heavy
body will gradually make room for

itself, and the lighter bodies in the pew will have to give up as the service goes on till at last Dives is comfortably settled.

Certainly the door was closed with an effort, and more than once during the service you heard it creak, and could not help hoping—but that was in the days of one's boyhood—that by some fortunate chance the door would one day give way, and Dives, who depended too utterly upon it, might be landed in the aisle. The hasp, however, not to say the hinges also, was strongly made, and the pew-opener saw that everything had been done for safety as well as dignity, and then he processed back again to the door, not unconscious that he had acquitted himself with credit and that he had created at least a sensation by his ceremonious disposal of the rich man and his family in their pew.

The Pew-Holder Made Himself Comfortable.

Dives unlocks the Bible box with a key which is upon his ring, and distributes the books as if he were presenting prizes to a school, while the mother of the family gives to its youngest members such provision in the way of sweets as will sustain exhausted nature through the next two hours.

There were cases where Dives was unmarried and had no other occupant for his mansion save his honorable self, but he was conducted in all the same, and set himself with dignity at the end of the lonely pew. And if you suppose that any stranger desiring a seat would be put in upon Dives, then you do not understand the discretion of the pew-opener; and if you imagine that a casual, dropping into that church, would himself try to break in upon that majestic vacancy, your imagination is bold enough, but it has not yet mastered the expression on Dives's face.

People Then Went to Their Own Churches.

Strangers did not in former days appear in churches unless they were guests with some of the families, because every one had his own church, and he went to it through rain or shine, whoever preached and whatever was going on either there or elsewhere. People boasted in those ancient times that they never wandered, and an absolute and unidentified stranger might have staggered the pew-opener, but being equal to any emergency, he would have conducted him to his own pew, which, for purposes of convenience, was near the pulpit, so that the wanderer might not interfere with any other person's property and might be under surveillance. There was an appearance of solidity

when the church was full, and of
respectability; there was also a suggestion of dignity and prosperity, and it is
right to add some flavor also of family
unity and homely comfort which was
most agreeable and comforting to that
old-time congregation.

Open-Handed Hospitality of the Modern Church.

If an old-fashioned person, and one,
perhaps, too much enamored of the past,
with all its faults, desires to receive
a shock, he has only to visit one of the
modern churches of the extreme type,
which are usually called free and open,
as if they were public houses or pieces
of waste ground on which rubbish is
landed. Openness has been carried to
its full length, for not only are there
no pew doors and no Bible boxes and no
cloth for your back and no cushion into
which you can sink—there may be a

mat and there may be hassocks—and hardly any division between one pew and another, but perhaps there are no pews at all, only chairs, and you stick your hymn-book into a rack in the back of your front neighbor's chair, who moves when you do so, and you kneel against that chair—if you are able to kneel at all—and then you push your front neighbor, which he naturally resents. Of course, there is no pew-opener, because there are no pew-doors to open, and more than that, there is no particular place for you to sit, because you can sit where you please and take a different seat at each service if you wish.

In the Church of To-day All Are Strangers.

No pilgrim nor stranger need be abashed in the modern church, for there is no other person there except people like himself; all are strangers, since they have no right to an inch of ground, and all are pilgrims, since they need not sit twice in the same place. No one can complain of any person's selfishness, since all things are held in common.

If Dives, locked within his door, suggested exclusiveness, it may be said for him it was the exclusiveness of home, and within the pew there was a little community—the original community of life, which is the family. And if something can be said for general free and openness on the ground of Christian brotherhood and human equality, one still clings to the belief that he is entitled to be with his own people—his wife, that is to say, and his children—in the House of God, and that he is more likely to worship God with reverence when he has some slight privacy.

The Family Existed Before the Pew.

Possibly a visitor may feel more liberty in a free and open church, but, on the other hand, the family is broken up into units at the door, and no mixed multitude can ever make so strong a congregation or one that appeals so powerfully to the eye as the long line of pews, let us say without doors and furniture, but each containing a family, with the mother at the head of the pew and the father at the foot and the young men and women between. For the family existed before the church, and if the church is not to be a mere possession of priests or a lecture hall, the church must rest on the family.

The pew is a testimony to the family, and ought to be maintained, with its doors removed, and it does not matter whether a man pay $50 a year for his pew or fifty cents. The church authorities should see that the householder

has his pew, with room enough in it for
himself, his wife, and the children
which God has given them. There is
no reason in the world why the rich
man should not pay a handsome sum
for his church home. And some of us
have never been able to understand why
an artisan should not give something
for his church home also. Surely every
man wishes to do what is right in the
support of his church.

Sunday Beggars and Monday Beggars.

Every self-respecting man likes to
pay for his home, whether it be large
or small, and it touches a man's honor
to live in a workhouse, where he pays
no rent and depends on the public.
There is no necessity that this home
feeling and this just independence
should be denied in the House of God,
but it rather seems a good thing that
the man who works and gives to pro-

vide a house where he and his children can live together in comfort and self-respect six days of the week should do his part to sustain the house where they worship God on the seventh day.

He is a poor creature who will allow a rich man to pay his rent for him on weekdays, and I have never been able to see where there is any difference between being a beggar on Sunday and a beggar on Monday.

POSSESSION OF A PEW IS A TEST OF CHARACTER.

One, however, wishes to add, and with emphasis, that the possession of a pew in the sense in which a man possesses his house is a test of character and an opportunity for hospitality. There is one kind of man who not only regrets that he cannot now have a door on his pew, but who would have it roofed in if he could, who will resent the introduction of a stranger—although there be plenty of room—as a personal affront, and will order strangers to be removed if, unhappily, they have been placed in his pew by mistake before he arrives. If he only occupy half a pew, the officers of the church dare not put in another set of tenants for the other half, because he will quarrel with them as to which half they are to occupy, as to who is to go in first, as to a hymn-book that has wandered out of its place, or about a friend they brought one day who infringed two inches upon his share of the pew. It is fair to say that the miscreant is no worse in church than he is elsewhere, for he is a churl everywhere—jealous, contentious, inhospitable, unmanageable.

One Man Whose Pew is Open and Free to All.

But, as a make-weight to this abuse of the pews, take my dear old friend

Jeremiah Goodheart. He is now alone
with his gentle, kindly wife, for the
children have made homes for themselves; but he keeps the family pew,
and will on no account give up a sitting.
It sometimes seems to the managers of
the church that Mr. Goodheart might
take a homeless family in, but they do
not press the matter when they remember how long he and his have had that
pew to themselves, and how well he uses
the vacant space. He has a number of
intimates who are now old and gray-
headed, and who come from time to
time to worship with him and his wife,
and feel that they are in right good
company. He has also an outer circle
of friends which can be numbered by
the hundred, and its members are also
in the habit of dropping in to sit in that
pew; and if he sees a stranger at the
church door, Goodheart must needs say
a word to him of welcome and good
cheer. If the stranger happen to be

a young man, he will take him by the
arm and bring him down to his pew,
and the chances are he will ask him
home to dinner and will tell him never
to sit alone in his lodgings, but to count
this house his home.

There is a Welcome Awaiting Him in Heaven.

And Mistress Goodheart tells her
friends with much satisfaction the size
of the joint they have on Sundays,
because, although their own sons have
gone, they never sit down without some
young men as guests, and Mr. Goodheart made their acquaintance through
the pew. If some family in the church
has visitors, and extra sittings are
needed, why, then, the children of the
family sit in the Goodheart pew and
are received with open arms. Bless his
white hair and genial face, he never is
entirely happy and never enjoys the

sermon unless he has his full contingent
of guests; and there are times when he
brings one too many, and then the other
pew-holders contend as to who shall
have him for their guest.

What he is in church he is at home,
with an open heart and an open hand,
never content unless his friends are
coming and going, never angry unless
they will not stay and have a meal with
him, never so full of joy as when he is
doing a good turn or going over old days
with those to whom he is bound by a
hundred ties of kindly words and deeds.
As he has dealt with all men, strangers
and friends alike, in his church and in
his house, so will God deal by him, and
for him we may feel sure there will be
a hospitable welcome waiting where the
churches of earth have changed into
Our Father's House.

VIII.

The Genteel Tramps in Our Churches.

IT is no exaggeration to say that the
use of money is a test of character and
a revelation of a man's nature. There
are men who lose money by their
foolishness—Wastrels; there are men
who spend it on their vices—Prodigals;
there are men who hoard it with jeal-
ousy—Misers; there are men who lay it
out in well-doing—they are the Wise
Men.

When I say well-doing I am not
thinking of that unreasoning and in-
discriminate charity which, whether it
take the form of alms to a lazy vaga-
bond or a large benefaction for the

creation of paupers, is a curse and not a blessing, a sin and not a duty. We are not to read in a mechanical fashion the advice of our Lord to the young ruler to sell his possessions and give to the poor, for though that might have been the only pledge of sincerity he could give in that day, it would be a great calamity in our day.

If a millionaire were to realize his estate and to bestow the proceeds upon that residuum of our population who will not work so long as they can beg, he would do the greatest injury within his power to his fellow-men. If the same person used his means to give the opportunity of honest work, whereby men could support themselves and their families, he would confer one of the greatest blessings in his power upon his fellow-men.

Whatever may have been the case in ancient times, there can be no question that in our day the man who establishes a manufactory in a small town and pays fair wages does ten times more good than he who would use his wealth to found an almshouse.

HEAD AS WELL AS HEART IS NEEDED IN GIVING.

When a man's family claims have been properly met, and his business enterprises have been soundly sustained, perhaps the best two things a man can do with his superfluous wealth is to use it to send the knowledge of God to those who sit in darkness, or to bestow the priceless gift of education upon those who hunger and thirst for knowledge. It is unfortunate that many persons have not learned to give, but it is also unfortunate that many people do not know where to give. The head as well as the heart is needed in giving, and giving is a training for one's brain as well as for one's feelings.

There are congregations which bring no intelligence to their giving, and for any good it does half their liberality had better have been flung into the sea. They keep up mission-houses in poor parts of the city, which are simply institutions for the propagation of pauperism, and the congregations they gather are largely made up of people who object to work between meals. Reports are published every year showing the number present at the services and containing harrowing accounts of the misery which has been relieved.

Congregations are Easy to Find.

As a matter of fact, if you give an able organizer $3000 a year to spend in a downtown district, he will secure you at any time a congregation of about five hundred people; and if the members of the mother church wish to go down and be present at an enthusiastic

meeting, then all that has to be done
is for one of its wealthy members to
play the host on that evening. The
gathering, both in numbers and enthusiasm, will leave nothing to be
desired, and the good people of the rich
church will go home feeling that they
have a flourishing mission and are
doing an immense deal of good, while
the chances are that they have really no
mission in the religious sense of the
word, and that their money has done
incalculable mischief.

Upon the whole, the mission churches
maintained on a principle of lavish
expenditure by rich congregations correspond exactly in their moral effect to
the almshouses founded by people who
have more money than they know what
to do with and not enough brains to
know how to use it.

Had the money squandered on soup
kitchens and clothing clubs and such
like schemes for the maintenance of

mendicants and their families been employed for the erection of a proper church, where honest people among the poor might worship God with self-respect, or of sanitary property, where working people might live in decency at moderate rents, or for the creation of a scholarship by which lads poor in money but rich in brains could obtain the higher education, then social reformers would have cause to bless the Church, and the Church would be a means of far greater good in the community.

When the Minister Has a Soft Heart.

A West End congregation does not, however, need to go to the East End to do mischief, for it can create, if it so please, a nursery of genteel tramps within its own borders. When a minister and his people have the reputation of a soft heart, and by that is often meant a soft head, the news spreads far and wide, and there is an immediate accession to the number of worshippers. Tradespeople of the lower class who wish to push their business and do not feel sufficiently confident about the goods they sell; young men who have lost their situations because they wouldn't do their work; families of women who would consider it beneath them to do anything for their own living and are adepts in what may be called genteel raiding; incapable men of business whom no bank would trust with $50, but who hope to get $1000 by quoting the Sermon on the Mount—all these gather and sit down within the sheltering walls of this Christian asylum.

They All Come to Benefit Themselves Financially.

They all come, according to their own story, for the most excellent and affecting reasons: because their last congregation was cold and they wished to live in a warmer atmosphere; because they have received benefit from the minister's preaching and feel it to be a privilege to be under his care; because they desire to do some good work, and have heard from afar of the zeal of this congregation; but chiefly on account of the spirituality, both of minister and people, which has been as a loadstone drawing these simple souls to their natural home. Their real reason, to put it in plain English, is that they do not care to work for their livelihood as honest folk do, and that they propose to cast themselves on congregational charity. They have come not because they care one cent what the minister preaches nor what he is, provided only he has no discernment, but simply and solely to beg. They are adepts in their own department, and have brought congregational begging to the height of

a fine art. They do not borrow as soon
as they arrive, and the more skilful
members of the craft will never mention
money at all. Their desire, as they
explain to the minister in his study
with a diffidence and a delicacy which
impress him very much if he be a man
of simple piety, is simply to have a
corner in his church where they can sit
and drink in the pure milk of the
Word; and their only trouble is that
for the first six months they will not
be able to pay any seat rent nor to give
any contribution to the missionary
funds.

They Talk of the Days When They Were Better Off.

There were days when they were
better off, they explain, and then the
delight of their life was liberality.
There has been a great family reverse,
and vague allusions are made to a large
sum lost either through the misconduct

of a relative or through the failure of a bank, and now they are compelled to live most economically. Their struggle, the minister is allowed to understand, is very keen; but it was not to talk about such things again to him, but only to assure him of the blessing he had been to them, and their anxiety to be useful members in his church. If they cannot give, they are at least willing to work, and generally by an accident choose a department of Christian service whose head is rich in this world's goods and known to be generous.

Under the eye of such a chief there is no end to the activity of our mendicant friends. They will offer to do anything. They will suggest new schemes of philanthropy; they will drive the old workers crazy by their fussing; and they will go some night, at an inconvenient hour, with half a dollar, which, it oozes out, they have saved for a good cause. As they are

not able to give to the church funds,
they make with their own hands some
preposterous offertory bags, which they
present formally to the office bearers of
the church, and which can never be
shown.

How They Distribute Their Trifling Gifts.

And as they have no other means of
proving their gratitude to the minister,
they call one evening, the man and his
wife together, who are colleagues in
mendicancy, and ask him to accept
a huge muffler, which will protect his
throat from the winter cold amid his
innumerable labors, and whose colors
and construction, if he wore the thing,
would render him liable to deposition
from the ministry. Leading members
of the congregation are faithfully re-
membered upon their birthdays and at
Christmas with cards emblazoned with
pious designs and observations; and if

a child be stricken with an anxious and
painful complaint like chicken-pox, the
inquiries of our mendicant friends are
regular and touching.   They do not like
to trouble the mother, but they have
conceived such an affection for the little
darling, whom they have watched in
church, that they couldn't rest without
learning whether the sweet pet had
passed a quiet day.   They do not wish
to be forward, and they do not forget
their changed circumstances, but they
hope it will not be considered an offence
to have brought just a trifle for the
angel in her sickness, and they ask the
mother to convey an unholy-looking
piece of candy to the little lamb.   There
are mothers and mothers, but the chances
are that the mother will be considerably
moved and, on the whole, well pleased
by this interest in her child, and although she will put the gift promptly
in the fire, she will not forget the givers
at Christmas time.

When They Have Spun Their Web Successfully.

When the spiders have spun their web of delicate filaments, and have stretched it from corner to corner of the church, it is amazing how many flies, not all of them simple, they have caught and how much spoil they have obtained. The wardrobes of the church, both of men and women, are at their disposal, and every month you are reminded of some old friend when you see our mendicant, and it is quite interesting to trace the "go-to-meeting" clothes of the congregation reappearing in new circumstances. Their house rent is paid, in turn, by a set of good Samaritans, each of whom believes that he is the only one who has ever been allowed to do this kindness, and who does it under promise of secrecy, lest shrinking natures, poor but proud, should be hurt, and that self-respect, which is now, as they explain, their only possession, should be destroyed. Some kindly doctor in the district gives his attendance, as is usual with those men, without money and without price. Medical comfort in the shape of cordials, jellies, fruit, delicate food, pour into the house with such a constant stream that it is not wonderful that dear little Alice does not recover quickly and that the assistance of the family has to be called in to use up the dainties.

Later, little Alice, who has been taken around, elaborately wrapped up and looking most piteous, to thank her benefactors in person, and who comes on most awkward occasions, has to be sent, through sheer pity, for a month into the country, and the fond family who cannot bear to live without little Alice—they never can quite shake off the habits of past prosperity—have to accompany the convalescent.

Borrowing From Every One They Meet.

Time would fail me to tell of the loans which they obtain from almost everybody, rich and poor. Which are asked in every case in circumstances of the last extremity and with a perfect agony of shame; which is the first money ever borrowed by the family, and is to be repaid in the course of fourteen days exactly; for which security is offered in the shape of an ancient gold brooch—the last heirloom of the family. It is only after the long raid has ended, and the mendicants have departed to another West End church at a safe distance, that people begin to compare notes and add up accounts, when it is discovered that at the lowest estimate the family have lived upon the congregation at the rate of $1000 a year.

This calculation is, of course, ex-

clusive of what they earn for themselves; but, as a rule, this would not
swell the balance. If any form of work
be suggested to the female mendicant
in reduced circumstances, she struggles
with her emotions, but cannot conceal
the fact that she is very much hurt. It
may be foolish, she explains amid her
tears, but her poor father, who has
generally been in the army, had often
said that no daughter of his name
should ever come to work, and she feels
it due to his memory to sustain this
noble attitude, and one is so much
ashamed at his brutal suggestion that
he willingly pays an indemnity.

WHEN THE MENDICANT IS A TRADES-MAN.

It is of no use attempting to get a
situation for a young fellow of this
tribe, since either the place you get for
him does not suit his peculiar ability, or

after he has been there for three days
there is a difference between him and
the manager of the office, which shows
that the manager has not been accustomed to deal with gentlemen; and, of
course, as the young man's mother tells
you, her son could not forget the history
of the family.

If the mendicant be a tradesman,
and you send him customers, for which,
indeed, he has been touting, the things
are so badly made that no one can wear
them, and the price is so high that no
one is inclined to pay it; and then
the tradesman generally belongs to that
high and mighty class which will not
condescend to make anything except in
the good old-fashioned way; and especially will not, even at the point of
starvation, lower the price. As a matter
of fact—naked fact—this high-spirited
tradesman does not want to work so
long as silly people will support him.

When the Minister's Eyes are Opened.

By and by even the kindliest of ministers, with the growth of intelligence in the Christian church, will see through this class, and will promptly subject them to a shrewd labor test, declining to mix up together piety and beggary, and refusing to believe that anybody has ever got any good from his ministry who will not work for his living. One also expects that a congregation of Christian people, the most credulous body on earth, will pluck up courage and at the same time rally their common-sense and refuse to make the Christian society a dumping-ground for genteel tramps, and the "Weary Williams" of religion will have to find out some new way of evading the law that if a man will not work, neither shall he eat.

And the money which has been saved
from these parasites might go to swell
the fund for the comfortable support
of retired ministers.

IX.

Is the Minister an Idler?

No man has more reason to be grateful to his public than a minister, for I know no servant who is more kindly treated. While there are, no doubt, in so large a body as the Christian Church censorious hearers and ill-mannered congregations, just as there are lazy and cantankerous ministers, yet the average congregation is charitable in its judgment of its minister, patient under his failings, keenly appreciative of any good work he does, and most responsive to all his good offices. There are not many substantial complaints which a

sane-minded and good-tempered minister can bring against the average congregation, but he has sometimes a
grudge against his friends which he
does not express, but which often
rankles in his heart. It is not anything
they say nor anything they do; it is
the quiet and perhaps unconscious
assumption on their part that he has
not enough work to do or that he has
a considerable quantity of time at his
disposal.

Were he to depend upon their words,
then this suspicion would never cross
his mind, because they have a trick,
and a kindly one, of saying to him on
Monday that he must be very tired
after preaching two such wonderful
sermons, and he, being only human, is
apt then to imagine that he is exhausted
after such an intellectual output.   At
other times they remonstrate with him
in a casual way, after the talk about
the weather, because he has been over-

working, and tell him that they cannot imagine how he is able to do so much. All this is friendly and comforting, and the minister has an agreeable sense that his work is appreciated, and that he is one of the austere toilers of the world.

The Minister's Time is Not Considered.

As he grows older, however, and begins to attach more importance to the attitude of a person's mind than the irresponsible words which fall from his lips, he has an uneasy sense that people are not so very much impressed by his exacting labors and his crowded hours. Delightful ladies, and all ladies are delightful, invite him to afternoon tea and such like functions, where he will be the only gentleman present; or if there be another, he will be an elderly man, long retired from business.

While the minister thanks the lady
for her thought of him, it comes to his
mind that her own husband will not be
at the pleasant little party nor her own
sons, because they are too busy, and she
would not dream of asking a barrister
or a merchant or a doctor or a journalist, unless it were some great affair to
which all society was going. It would
seem to her absurd to take a busy man
away ·from his work, even to spend an
hour with her and other equally charming women. The other men would not
come because they could not. They
must do their work. The minister is
invited because, as his hostess assumes,
he has no work to prevent his coming.
And she would be apt to consider him
somewhat less than courteous, and certainly not obliging, if he refused; and
if he did so on account of his time
being occupied, even her charity might
fail her, and she might allow herself to
think that he had some other reason.

Was he not sitting in his study? Why might he not as well be in her house? And she would never understand it was his only chance that afternoon of mastering a necessary book. Had he not passed her house half an hour before, and if he could go out for a walk, why might he not have spent the time in her garden, and he cannot explain to her that he was going to visit a case of sickness.

Secretaries of philanthropic societies will ask him to go down from a distant suburb to the heart of the city, and second a resolution at a public meeting of eight elderly gentlemen and seventy-seven females of uncertain age, together with four genteel mendicants who have come to see whether they can borrow five shillings from some good Samaritan.

Faddists of All Sorts Harass the Minister.

It was an excellent society, and it was necessary its committee should be re-elected, and the minister said so at the length of ten minutes, but the bitter question was in his heart as he went home, tired and fretted: Was this the best use he could make of his time, and would the secretary, indefatigable though he was and full of push, have asked a business man—that is, a man really busy—to have left his office in the heat of the work and spend three hours of his time in going out to a suburb and saying what was of no importance to people on whom it would have no special effect? The minister knows, and the secretary knows, and everybody knows that the business man would have said no in the shortest form of words, and no person would have been indignant that he should say so,

and every person would have held him
to be a foolish man if he had gone.

Such an expenditure of time is
impossible except for superannuated
gentlemen and for ministers. And, of
course, if ministers are simply fiddling
away their time in the house reading
magazines or looking out at the windows, or if they are only gadding
around their districts paying compli-
mentary calls and talking about the
weather, it would be a good thing, if
only for a change, that they should
spend an afternoon going and coming
to a meeting and convincing the audience that they ought to re-elect the
committee.

Faddists of every description drop
into a minister's study, preferring the
forenoon, because they are sure to find
him at home, and explain to him at
enormous length that we are the descend-
ants of the lost ten tribes; that moral
evils would be largely done away with

if we ate carrots instead of meat; that
the work carried on by some person
whose name the minister can't pro-
nounce, at a place in Asia Minor of
which he never heard, and on the sole
responsibility of the man who draws
the salary in Asia Minor, is the most
important in the range of foreign missions.   Were any one of these voluble
people, and they are only three out of a
hundred, each with a bee in his bonnet,
to visit a merchant's office, he would not
likely be allowed into the principal's
room, and if he were, he would soon
again be in the outer office.

The effrontery of a faddist is amazing, but it has limits; and after a little
experience the faddist leaves the merchant alone, and, as a rule, he does not
even attempt the doctor, but he settles
down as by an instinct and with a feeling of being at home in the minister's
study.   If the minister be a really good
man, the faddist enjoys himself very

much, for he has got a helpless victim; but if the minister be an imperfectly sanctified man, then the faddist goes to the door almost as quickly as from the merchant's room, but the minister knows that his life is in the power of the faddist's tongue.

MINISTERS HAVE LITTLE TIME FOR THEMSELVES.

What annoys the minister, and all the more so that he cannot express his annoyance, is that all those people believe that he does not really know what to do with his time, and that it is at every person's disposal. As a matter of fact, the conscientious minister of a city church works harder than any person in the community, except a doctor in general practice, a journalist on a daily paper, and a seamstress under the sweater's lash. He may sit as late as he please at night—and, indeed, must sit till, say, midnight at least—in order to keep up with his reading, but he must be up early in the morning, because a business man will come in to see him before nine o'clock, and by that time he must have opened his first mail, which will amount to about twelve letters, and if he thinks it necessary—and in a city it is necessary—must have gathered at a glance what happened yesterday in his community and in the world. From nine to one he is at work preparing for the pulpit, for week-night services, for classes, and for miscellaneous church and public work, as hard as he can, and the hour which he loses through callers has to be made up with interest late at night. He allows himself some food at one o'clock, although very often he has to take it cold, because some ingenious beggar knows that is the best time to find him, and in the height of the season he grudges the loss of his meal-time, and longs for the day when

American invention, fertile in ideas and parsimonious of time, will invent a liquid food which he can take in from a pipe while he is studying.

WHEN HE RETURNS HOME AFTER A BUSY DAY.

If he has not promised to second the appointment of a committee of forty members to manage a home for twenty girls, then he spends the time from about two to six visiting people who are sick, or who have lost friends, or who are in religious anxiety, or who are suffering worldly loss, or who have just come to his church, or who are just leaving his church, or whom he wishes to enlist for work, or whom he has not seen for some time and desires to keep in touch with. He returns home in the evening, not because his work is done, because this kind of work is never done and never can be done, even if he began at

nine in the morning and continued till
nine at night, but because no man can
stand more than five hours of visiting.

Upon his return—and I confess this
frankly—the minister allows himself
a little more food, but again it has to
be kept for him, because another visitor
who has missed him in the afternoon
discovers from a guileless waitress, who
has just come to the minister's house
and has not yet learned the duties of
a minister's servant, the hour at which
the unfortunate man will get his next
meal, and has been waiting for half an
hour to ask the help of the minister for
a cause which in two cases out of three
is a mere excrescence upon philanthropy, and a cause with which the
minister has not the remotest connec-
tion.

People who do not know might suppose that after the minister had taken
his very modest meal he would be at
liberty to sit with his wife and children

in the family room and discharge one of his duties as the head of the household as well as to enjoy the sweetest pleasure of the day. It is a rare thing that this unfortunate man has an evening to himself, because immediately after dinner he has to go to a service or to a meeting at his church, and while the members of the congregation distribute themselves among the different evenings, which is quite right, he must be present at everything, or if he is not, then that from which he is absent begins to fail.

WHEN HE HOPED FOR AN EVENING TO HIMSELF.

If he has an evening to spare, then some member of his congregation will ask him to come to a meeting on behalf of something or other in which he is interested, and there are reasons why the minister cannot refuse. Likely as not that very gentleman had been saying

last week that the minister was over-
worked and must not make so many
engagements, but when the time comes
that he has an axe of his own to grind
he will not have the slightest hesitation
in asking the minister to turn the
grindstone. And indeed the public
work of the minister is much increased
by his own people, who give the secretaries and the faddists and the rest of
the brigands letters of introduction
which conclude, " I hope you will grant
Mr. Tootle's request as a personal favor
to myself." The same gentleman may
only do this once in six months, but
then a hundred other people in the
church will do the same at intervals,
and so the minister is sold into bondage
by those of his own household.

WHY HE SELDOM HAS AN EVENING TO HIMSELF.

Were I a layman, and some paid
secretary who has nothing else to do—

as it sometimes appears to me—except
to write unnecessary letters and get up
wearisome meetings and harass ministers, came to me and asked me to tease
my minister into leaving his own work
and attending the secretary's meeting,
I would express my mind to the secretary in the language which might be
given me in that hour by a kindly
Providence, and one minister at least
would be saved from the secretary. If
the religious public has ever any mis-
giving about the money which is spent
on secretaries, and the usefulness of
their work, it may be some consolation
for that public to know that as long as
there are paid secretaries for philanthropic societies, no city minister will
ever be allowed to idle away his time,
either in reading modern theology or in
talking with his family.

Suppose, however, that by some
extraordinary mercy the minister has
an evening to himself, actually to him-

self—which will come about six times
in the winter season—and he proposes
to read aloud to his wife, or that she
should give him a little music, or that
the family should look over some art
books together, or—for I am not hiding
his little weaknesses—that they should
play a game together, his wife, his
children, and himself.   The bell rings,
and the minister looks at his wife; he
knows what that means.   It is at such
moments that his belief in a personal
devil, whose ingenuity is in keeping
with his malignancy, is firmly established.

Neither His Time Nor His Privacy Respected.

It is not that the caller would naturally suggest Satan to a stranger, for
he is simply a respectable, not very
brilliant, citizen, belonging to the minister's congregation or perhaps to some
other   minister's   congregation,   who

might have called at some other hour,
and would have called at another time
if he had wished to see a merchant, but
who breaks in upon the minister's
privacy with the vague idea in his mind
that as the minister had all the day to
himself, his evening hours are at the
mercy of the public. As regards the
visitor's errand, he might as well have
written, but he felt it would be better
discussed at a personal interview—fifteen minutes would give ample opportunity. As it is, this garrulous
gentleman sits down for the evening in
the minister's study, and when he goes,
full of regret for having occupied so
much of the minister's time, the children have gone to bed and the minister's
wife is sitting lonely in the empty
drawing-room.

There is no other man who suffers
after this fashion, not even a doctor, for
people do not saunter in and sit in his
consulting-room when they ought to be

with their families, and he wishes to be
with his. Doctors have a hard life, for
they are liable to be called out at any
hour and to be worked from morning
till night, but they are at least pro-
tected from casual visits and twaddling
conversation by the simple fact that if
a man comes to their consulting-room,
he is not allowed to stay longer than
fifteen minutes, and he has to pay for
the time he stays. Of course, a minister
is at the service of his congregation at
all reasonable hours, and at any hour
he is ready for the service of the
dying and bereaved; but if every
stranger who has no claim upon him,
and who comes to him about his own
affairs, had to pay a reasonable fee, and
this fee were doubled if he came in the
evening, then a minister's children
might come to know their father and
a minister's wife would not have to
complain that she saw hardly anything
of her husband.

MINISTERS NEED TIME TO REST AND THINK.

When a merchant leaves his office and goes to his home he would be astounded if a cotton broker called and proposed to do business. A working-man has rest in his own home, but a minister's home is a thoroughfare along which all kinds of people travel. Why should not a minister's home be as sacred as that of a merchant? Why should he not have his periods of daily rest as much as the barrister? When will it be understood by congregations and by the public that if a man is to keep abreast with the thought of the day, and master the best thought of the past, if he is to discharge aright his pastoral duties and take his proper part in the greater movements of the commonwealth, his time must be guarded from intrusion and his energies gathered in from the dissipation

of petty meetings ?   When will people
understand that his work is as serious
and as exacting as that of any other
professional man, and that while his
time belongs unto his Master, as well
as his talents and everything he possesses, it does not belong to paid officials
and garrulous callers ?   When that is
clearly understood, then it will dawn
for the first time on certain minds that
while the minister has many functions
to perform, one of them is not to be the
substitute in society for busy men or
a talking machine at second-rate religious meetings.

X.

The Minister and His Vacation.

There is no wholesome and sensible
minister who does not wish to have the
good will of every class in his congregation, but he especially covets the respect
and confidence of the young men. This
is not because they are wiser than their
elders nor because they are more spiritual, but because they are unconventional
and sincere to the last degree.

A woman, on account of her goodness
and reverence, will respect a minister
because of his office; a young man will
only respect him because of himself.
If the minister be unreal, shifty, cow-
ardly, or lazy, then although he had

been ordained twelve times and is as
eloquent as Apollos and has a melting
pulpit voice and a charming private
manner, young men will see through him
and despise him and have nothing to do
with him, and will refuse to go to church
on his account, while, on the other hand,
although the minister be not very clever
and cannot preach deep sermons and
has a habit of talking plainly and does
not know many religious parlor tricks,
if he be straight and hard working and
fearless in thought as well as deed, they
will go to hear what he has to say and
will stand up for him when his back is
turned and will drop in to see him in
his study and will consult him when
they have got into a scrape. They are
not judges of sanctity, and are apt to
depreciate really good men because they
are sometimes weakly and effeminate,
but they are infallible judges of manli-
less, and, above all things, they believe
in a manly minister. They do not ask

that he should play games, for he may
be growing old or he may be crippled in
body, but they do ask that he play the
game of life bravely and honorably.

The true minister is perfectly satisfied to be judged by the young men's
standard—how he plays the big game
—but he is sometimes concerned because young men think that at one point
he has a special advantage, and he is
the last man to desire favors on the
field. He does not want to be shielded
from criticism nor to be given into on
account of his position nor to be petted
in any fashion, but to do his work and
take his chances and suffer his reverses
and fight his battle like any other man.
And, therefore, the minister is justly
sensitive about one subject of criticism,
and that is his holidays.

Last summer, let us suppose, he was
spending the month of August in the
country, doing nothing worth mentioning, except walk and climb and fish and

golf and drive and ride and fifty other things he did when he was a boy. He had earned his holiday by eleven months' preaching, teaching, studying, presiding, advising, comforting, rebuking, visiting, organizing, and fifty other things he never thought he would ever come to do when he was a boy. His conscience was quite at ease at the close of the day, though he had not written a word, because there was no sermon to preach on Sunday; and though he had not visited a person, because there was not a person to visit, and he congratulated himself because through the length of the long idle days he was gathering strength of body and reviving his mind for his winter's work.

A Visitor Who Was Warmly Welcomed.

One evening a bicycle came along the lonely road at full pace and pulled up

at the gate, and through the garden
came a rider, clad in light undress,
bareheaded, his face burned to a choco-
late color, covered with dust, pleasantly
tired with his spin of forty miles, but
full of health and strength and glad-
ness. He challenged the minister to
tell the truth as between man and man
whether he knew him.

Knew him! Upon the whole, and
making a virtue of truthfulness, the
minister admitted that he did, for this
was the young fellow who sat at the end
of the front seat in the transept on
Sunday mornings, and on Sunday evenings kept order in an East End school
for boys, and was always ready to look
after some other young fellow, and was
as good a sort of man as could be made.

He was taken with triumph and
shouting into the cottage, and after a
wash and a stupendous meal the minister and he wandered along the hillside
and talked about many things, and came

back and sat in the garden amid the
smell of the flowers, till they could no
longer speak for sleep. In the morning
they climbed the hill behind and viewed
the country, and then the young man
went on his way, and at the corner of
the road he said farewell; and as he did
so he mournfully shook his head, for he
was making for the nearest railway sta-
tion, and the next day he would be hard
at work in the hot city. " My last day,"
he said to the minister as they parted,
" and it has been a jolly one," and although the young man did not grudge
the minister the extra fortnight he was
going to have, the minister could not
help feeling that they had not parted on
equal terms, but that he was thought to
have the best of it.

COUNTING UP THE VACATION DAYS.

When that happy summer day had
become only a pleasant memory and

winter held the land, the two were sitting together again in the minister's study—this time before the blazing logs. They were talking of many things—among others that garden with its wealth of carnations—and the minister charged the young man with his secret thought, and declared that he believed every young man had the same idea in the background of his mind. It was agreed to have a debate there and then, and the minister undertook to prove that he had fewer holidays than a clerk in an office, and that not for the sake of arguing a ridiculous position, but because he believed it to be the truth. The young man was delighted to take the opposite side.

It was indeed a simple question of arithmetic to put two sets of figures down upon a sheet of paper and subtract the lesser from the greater number; the balance left would decide the debate.

As the minister had a city parish and a considerate congregation, he was more generously treated than many of his brethren, and was allowed in the course of the year a six weeks' holiday, which he divided into a month at the close of summer, and a fortnight in the spring-time, when the heavy work of winter had been finished. And this made forty-two days. Between January and December he very occasionally had a day in the country outside holiday times, or half a day in the city, wherein he followed his own pleasure. The country day very often meant golf, and the city half-day, hunting through a library and prowling among the book-shops. Let such odds and ends be set down in all at eight days, and the minister's vacation amounted to fifty days.

WHEN THE TOTAL WAS WRITTEN DOWN.

When the minister himself wrote down the total his opponent felt that it was hardly worth stating his case. As the minister insisted and furnished the young man with a sheet of paper and a pencil the debate seemed to grow into a comedy.

"Twelve days is the rule in our office, and one is lucky if he gets away in August, for he may be put off with April," said the young man. And he was already deducting twelve from fifty and wondering what the minister would say to a majority of thirty-eight.

"Does your furlough," questioned the minister, "include Sundays in the twelve days?" The young man admitted it did not. And so the figure twelve was changed to fourteen, but that did not make any great difference.

"Is your office open on Christmas

Day ?" continued the minister. " I
think not; nor on New Year's Day, nor
Easter Monday, nor Whit Monday. By
the way, unless I am mistaken you
have the day after Christmas, too, and
another day at Easter time. We are
coming along nicely; that makes six
days you had not reckoned, and then
there is a bank holiday about the beginning of August, which you avoid when
you are arranging your yearly holiday.
Where are we now ? Twenty-one days,
I declare—three weeks. It is little
enough for a man who works so hard,
but it is better than you had reckoned."

" Yes, it reduces your majority, but
it still stands at a respectable figure—
twenty-nine days more to the minister
than to the clerk."

" Perhaps," replied the minister,
" but what a shameful thing it is that
your firm, which has such a good name
and does such a large business, should
work their clerks the whole of Saturday

instead of giving them a good half holiday. Nothing, I should say, would be more pleasant for a young fellow than to be able to take a run into the country on his bicycle on Saturday afternoon, when the flowers are just beginning to come out and the hedgerows have their first green, or to have four hours' skating through clear, clean, bracing winter air. I pity you," said the minister with sympathy, "not having the Saturday half holiday. You are as badly off as I am myself, to whom Saturday is the second hardest day of the week."

WHEN THE MINISTER ENVIES THE LAYMAN.

The minister arose and threw another log upon the fire, for he was a generous man and also had some sense of humor, and did not wish to put his friend to confusion.

"Never thought of that," said the

young man ingenuously; " it is quite true. I remember pitying you one day when I was going to skate and came in to see whether you would go with me, and found you grinding at your second sermon."

" Well," said the minister, " half a day for fifty-two weeks comes to twenty-six whole days, and deducting the two half holidays counted into your regular vacation, that leaves twenty-five days to be added to the twenty-one, which makes forty-six, unless my poor head is wrong in the addition.

" Oh ! " said the minister, " I am right, am I ? You stand now forty-six against my fifty. I must congratulate you upon your minority. No minister complains of his work, not even of the push and anxiety of Saturday, but I tell you honestly, Dick, there are times when he envies a layman his Sunday, for the Sunday is the layman's day of rest and the minister's day of toil. On

that day most people have a little longer
sleep in the morning—though very likely you rise at five o'clock on Sunday
morning to study Hebrew—and then
they have a leisurely breakfast—for why
should they hurry, it is not a working
day? Between breakfast and church
time they talk about all kinds of things
and turn over books and read letters
that have come from abroad, and have
the sense of being at their ease. If it
be fair weather they take the longest
road to church, walking through a garden or a park, and they saunter church-
ward with unembarrassed minds. The
father sits with his family in their pew
and can give his mind to the worship
without distraction and without fear.
Perhaps he never thinks about the minister's wife, who sits like a widow in
her pew with her children as orphans,
for the head of her household is that
day on his hardest duty, and has so
much to do in leading other people's

worship that he can hardly be said to have rest enough of mind to worship himself. Please don't interrupt," for the young man was beginning to ask terms of surrender.

Once the Minister Had a Sunday to Himself.

"Do you know," said the minister as he looked into the dancing firelight, "that some years ago I had a Sunday to myself with my family, and I can still taste its sweetness. We started discussions on Bible characters and religious subjects after breakfast, and I found out for the first time what my boys were thinking about. We hunted up books which had been mentioned, and I read favorite passages from the poets and showed rare editions and bits of binding which I kept locked up from the light and dust. We gossiped, we loitered, we hung over treasures. We took tea in the garden, we talked of old days, we made plans for the future. Why, I walked with my family to church, with no weight on my mind and no reason for hurry. So keenly did I enjoy the day that I resolved to taste it to the last drop.

" Do you think I went into the vestry before service because it was my vestry, and instructed the minister about the notices because it was my church? Certainly not. I went in through the front door, like any other member of the congregation, and nodded affably to the officials as I passed. I walked up the aisle behind my family and sat at the end of my pew like any other head of a household. After service I did go to the vestry, and having been admitted, thanked the preacher for his sermon as one of his hearers, and then went home talking about the service with my boys, for it was another man's sermon and I could enlarge upon its good points.

That afternoon, having time at my disposal, I visited a hall downtown where a man with a gift of his own was teaching two hundred unskilled laborers the elements of religion, and came home mightily refreshed, and then we read again and talked, and my family and I became almost intimate, because we had leisure and it was Sunday.

" At evening service I had the pleasure of picking up a young man at the door who was waiting for a seat, and taking him to my pew, and explaining to him that he might always have that seat in the evening, and that I was glad he had come, as we were going to have a good sermon. He looked curiously at me, and was about to say something when I anticipated him and explained that I was not the minister of the church that day, but simply a hearer like himself. I had more talk with my family after service—the pleasant rambling but not unprofitable conversation of people who were not tired nor over-strung, and so the day of rest closed in kindly fellowship and inward peace. We must all make sacrifices, Dick, but the hardest one that a minister has to make is his Sunday, for it is to the injury of his own soul and also of his family. Be thankful for your quiet Sundays and guard them jealously for the rest of mind and body."

"You have proved your case," said Dick; "adding fifty Sundays and twenty-five half Saturdays, I make my vacation ninety-six days against your fifty."

THERE IS NO END TO THE CHURCH WORK.

"It is mean," said the minister, "to triumph over a beaten foe, especially when he is such a good fellow, but figures cannot quite represent the case, because there is the question of the

different kind of work done, say, in an
office and in a study. I know that
business is exacting, that it means a
steady grind, and that it is full of sur-
prises and disappointments and the
chance of great reverses, but the business man has his own advantages. For
one thing, there is a limit to his work,
and when he comes home in the evening
he leaves his work behind him. But
there is no limit whatever to the minister's work. It is ever hanging over
him, ever distracting his thoughts, ever
exasperating his nerves, ever reproach-
ing his conscience. When he allows
himself a social evening, he does not
meet with the other guests on equal
terms, because they have written their
last letter and discharged their last
duty for the day, and when they go
home it will be to finish the last chapter
of a pleasant book and go to bed; but he
tore himself away from half-finished
work, and when his friends are sleeping

the light will be burning on his desk.
Besides—and, Dick, you cannot imagine
what this means—the merchant knows
that he can do so much work in eight
hours, because he is dealing with affairs;
but the minister never knows what he
can do, because he is dealing with ideas.
It is the necessity of production, even
when the mind will not produce, which
grates upon the nerves of a minister
and is apt to break down his health.

"The journalist writes every day,
but he has something new to write
about; the literary man writes when he
is inclined; the minister has to write
on an old subject—although the greatest which can engage the mind—and he
has to write whether his mind is bright
or dull. Possibly no man has moments
of such joy—when he is inspired; certainly no man has such hours of depres-
sion—when he has fallen beneath his
subject. It is only by patient reading
and unceasing prayer that he can

accomplish his duty, and then he is ever strained to the utmost, and never knows the rest of the man who does his work with time and strength and ideas to spare. When the minister in active service lies down to die he will be giving directions in his last conscious moments about a letter that had not been answered, and sending explanations to a family that has not been visited, and when his mind begins to wander, it will be among texts with which he has struggled and efforts which he has made in vain."

Longer Vacations Should be the Rule.

" He ought to have two months every year," cried Dick, " and when I am a deacon I'll see that my minister has a six months' holiday in addition every seven years, in order that he may begin again as a new man in mind and body."

" You are a good fellow, Dick, and you're wise for your years, and if the Church treated her ministers after this fashion she would reap all the gain. For every new idea which comes to the minister's mind, and every new book he reads, and every new sight he sees, and every new gallery he visits during his holidays pass into his words and into his life, and the thoughtfulness and generosity of congregations would come back to their own souls with usury of reward."

XI.

The Revival of a Minister.

It was not that the minister had become too old, for he was still in the prime of life; or that his health had failed, for he was stronger than in the days of his youth; or that he had ceased to study, for he was a harder reader than ever; or that he had lost touch with the age, for he was essentially a modern thinker. It was not that he was less diligent in pastoral work or less skilful in organization, nor was it that he had quarrelled with his congregation, or his congregation with him, nor was it that the district had changed or that the church had been left without people.

He preached as well as ever he did, and
with much more weight and wisdom
than twenty years ago. There were as
many members on the roll, and as much
money raised, and as much work done,
and the church had as great a reputation. It was difficult to lay your finger
upon anything wanting in minister or
people, and yet the minister was conscious and the people had a vague sense
that something was wrong. The spirit
of the congregation was lower, their discharge of duty was flatter, their response
to appeals was slower, their attendance
at extra services was poorer. There
was less enthusiasm, less spontaneity,
less loyalty. After fifteen years of service in the same place, addressing the
same people, and saying, of necessity,
the same things, and moving about in
the same district, the minister, without
any fault on his part, but simply
through an infirmity of human nature,
had grown a little weary. He had lost

freshness, not of thought nor of expression, but of spirit; and there was not in him now that buoyancy of soul and that hopefulness of tone and that perpetual joy of speech which once had attracted people and won their hearts. And, on their part, the people had lost freshness toward him; not respect for him nor gratitude for his past service nor appreciation of his present work, but their sense of expectation from him and their affectionate delight in him and their joy in speaking about him. Their pulses were not stirred when he preached, nor did a visit from him make an event, nor would his absence make any great blank in their lives. There was still an honest affection between the minister and his people, but it had lost the passion and romance of past years. It was now undemonstrative and well regulated; perhaps a trifle too sober and calm to be called affection.

The people had grown so accustomed
to their minister, his appearance, his
voice, his way of thinking, his tricks
of manner, that they were able to criticise him and note his faults with much
accuracy. He did not care to be contra-
dicted, and was apt to be irritated when
his plans were opposed ; he was too fond
of certain lines of thought, and did not
always preach to edification ; he was
apt to be too much with a few friends,
and did not hold himself sufficiently at
the disposal of all ; he gave too much
attention to outside work, and sometimes neglected his pastoral duty ; he
insisted upon using his leisure time as
he pleased, and did not seem to remember that he ought not to have had any
leisure time ; he was apt to grumble
when extra duties were put upon him,
and was not always gracious when asked
to do more than his own work. Ten
years ago no one had dared to hint at
those faults, for he would have been

torn in pieces by his fellow-members, as
an evil-minded and unreasonable man.
The minister was very much then what
he is now, but his faults then were lost
in high spirits and earnestness and
kindly feeling and devotion to spiritual
duty. He was perfect then in the
glamour of the morning light; he is an
ordinary man now whose imperfections
are clearly seen in the glare of noonday.
The minister is also able now to look at
his people from a distance and to judge
them with an impartial mind, while
once they were to him altogether lovely,
without spot or blemish or any such
thing, and you might have more safely
criticised a bride's appearance to her
bridegroom during the honeymoon than
have found fault with this man's congregation. Whether it be that his eyes
are clearer or his heart is colder, he is
under no delusions now; and although
he would not say such things in public,
he knows quite well wherein his people

come short. Some of them are hope-
lessly bigoted in their own views, and
are not open even to the best light,
which he is apt to think is his own.
Some of them are so liberal that they
have hardly any faith, and he forgets
to remind himself that for their lack of
faith he is responsible. Some of them
are so worldly that the highest appeals
of religion have no effect upon their
lives, and some of them so ungenerous
that they will hardly support the best
of causes. He feels keenly that young
people whom he trained and loved are
no longer true to him, but prefer other
voices, and are as enthusiastic about
others as once they were about him; and
he misses little acts of kindness, which
are no longer rendered him, and which
he valued, not for their own value, but
because they were the sacraments of
friendship. He still believes his congregation to be better than any other
he knows, he still remembers their

loyalty in years past; but the days of
first love are over, and his heart is
sometimes heavy.

One evening the office bearers of the
church had been meeting, and when
the business was done they drifted into
talk about the church life and about
their minister. They were, upon the
whole, a body of honorable, sensible,
good-hearted, and straightforward men,
who desired to do their best by their
minister, and not to vex him in any
way; who always took care that he had
a proper salary and a good holiday;
who would never complain without
reason, and who would never dream of
asking any man to resign, and setting
him adrift after a long service without
a pension. But they were not satisfied
with the state of affairs, and after much
talking up and down, suggesting, hint-
ing, indicating, qualifying, it was
almost a relief when Mr. Judkin, their

chairman, and a strong man in word and deed, gave expression to their minds.

"There is no man," he said, "I respect more thoroughly than our minister, for he has worked hard and made our congregation what it is. He is well read and a good preacher, and no one can say a word against his life or conduct; but there is no question, and I think it is better that it should be said instead of being felt in secret, that somehow or other our minister is losing his hold upon the people, and that the congregation is not what it used to be in tone and in heart. My impression, brethren, is that while it might be a risk for us, and very likely we would never get any one who could do for us what our minister has done in the past, that he has finished his work and both sides would be better to have a change." And when Mr. Judkin looked round he saw that he had been understood, and was encouraged to continue to the end.

" Our minister has so good a position in the church and his reputation is so high that he could easily obtain another congregation if he wished. In fact, I have reason to believe that he has had opportunities of making a change, but has always refused to entertain the idea. There is no man in the congregation who would ask the minister to leave— certainly I shall not; but I am not sure but that a new beginning would be the best thing for the minister, and also, I am bound to add, might be a good thing for us. One thing I would like to say more, and that is about the finance. We are not a poor church and we will always be able to pay our way, but we have a pretty heavy debit balance, and there was rather a poor response to the last appeal from the pulpit. If the congregation were in good heart, the necessary $2000 could have been got in a week."

There was a pause, during which

several brethren conveyed by looks and nods to Mr. Judkin that he had expressed their mind; and then the silence was broken by Mr. Stonier, who was distinguished in the congregation and outside of it by extreme parsimony in money matters, an entire absence of sentiment, and a ghastly frankness of speech. It was felt when he took up the speaking, that if Mr. Judkin had placed the nail in position, Mr. Stonier would hammer it in to the head, but you never can tell. "This," said Mr. Stonier, "is a conference, I suppose, when any man can say anything he pleases, and there are no rules of order. For myself, I did not know that we were going to sit to-night in judgment on the minister, and I didn't know that Mr. Judkin and the rest of you were going to ask him in some roundabout, gentlemanly, Christian, high-toned fashion to look out for another place. Oh, yes; that is just what you are after, but you are such a set of pussy-cats that you won't speak out and say what you mean! For myself, I've been a seat-holder in the church for fifteen years, and when I came here the church was nearly empty, and now it's quite full, and the minister has done fifteen years' hard work. Now, I do not set up to be a philanthropist, and I never gave a penny for the "conversion of the Jews," nor to the "Society for Supplying Free Food to Street Loafers," nor to any other of the schemes you gentle-men advocate. I am not what is called a large giver, but I hope I'm an honest man; and I tell you that if I had a man in my office who had served me fifteen years and done his work well, and I proposed to get rid of him because I was tired seeing the same man always at his desk and the same writing in the ledger, I should consider myself a scamp; and I thank God I never have done such a thing with any of my staff.

If you can find any man who has been in my office and been dismissed because I wanted to see a new face, then I'll give $100 to Timbuctoo or any other mission you like." No one expected to earn the prize, for it was well known that although Mr. Stonier was as hard as nails to miscellaneous charity, he was an excellent master in his own office.

"As regards the deficit in the church funds, if that is the ground on which the minister is going to be dismissed, I'm prepared to pay the whole sum myself; and I do it, mark you, as a token of respect and gratitude—gratitude, see you, gentlemen, for fifteen years' honest work." No sooner had this outspoken man sat down than Mr. Lovejoy, the kindest and sweetest soul in all the congregation, who had been very restless for some time, ventured on speech.

"I do not wish to argue with my dear brethren who have spoken, for Brother

Judkin is too strong for me, and no person could reply to Brother Stonier with his handsome offer. Most generous, and just like his kind heart, of which I have had experience for many years in my little charities; but that's a secret between Brother Stonier and me. What I want to say is that I love our minister for what he is and for what he was to me in the time of my great sorrow. When . . . I lost my beloved wife he brought the Lord's consolation day by day to my heart, and our pulpit will never be the same to me without our minister." And that was all that Mr. Lovejoy said.

It seemed, however, to touch a hidden spring in every one present, and one after another the office bearers spoke. They seemed to have forgotten the matter before them and the delicate suggestion of Mr. Judkin. One rose to say that the minister had married him, and he never could forget the marriage address; another had lost a little lad quite suddenly, and he did not think that his wife and he could have endured the trial had it not been for the minister's sympathy; a third had passed through worldly trials, and it was the minister's sermon that had kept him above water; and a fourth, who, as every one knew, had passed through fearful temptation, wished humbly to testify that he had not been that night an office bearer in a Christian church without the minister's help in time of trouble. Others looked as if they could have spoken, several murmured sympathy, and one deacon surreptitiously used his handkerchief, and at last Mr. Judkin rose again and proved himself a man worthy to lead and to guide a church.

"Brethren," he said, "I expressed the feeling that was in my mind, and I am thankful that I gave it expression, for it has relieved me, and it has done

good to you.   I now withdraw what I
said : I was a little discouraged. Brother
Stonier is quite right, and he has braced
us up; and if he clears off the deficit, for
which we are all much obliged, I shall
be very glad if you allow me, brethren, to
repaint the church this fall, for the colors are getting a little faded, and I would
like to do it as a sign of gratitude for
what the minister was to my wife when
our son was hanging between life and
death."   Mr. Judkin's example set the
office bearers upon a new track, one
offering to supply the Sunday-school
with new hymn-books, about which
there had been some difficulty; another
declaring that if the mother church was
going to be repainted, he would see that
the mission church should also get
a coat; a third offered to pay the
quarter of a missionary's salary to take
the burden off the minister's shoulders,
and three other office bearers appro-
priated the remaining quarters, till at

last there was not a man who had not
secured the right, personal to himself,
of doing something, great or small, for
the church, and every one was to do it
out of gratitude to the minister for all
he had been to them and all he had done
for them during fifteen years. And
finally Mr. Lovejoy melted all his
brethren by a prayer, in which he carried both minister and people to the
Throne of Grace, and so interceded that
every one felt as he left the place that
the blessing of God was resting upon
him.

The week-night service was held on
Wednesday, and, as a rule, was very
poorly attended. On this week the
minister had come down to his vestry
with a low heart, and was praying that
he might have grace to address Mr.
Lovejoy and a handful of devout and
honorable women without showing that
he was discouraged himself and without
discouraging them. There were days

in the past when the service had been
held in the church, and Mr. Judkin
used to boast in the city about the attendance; and then it descended from
the church to the large hall; but of late
the few who attended had been gathered
into a room, because it was more cheer-
ful to see a room nearly full than a hall
three parts empty. The room was next
door to the vestry, and the minister
could tell before he went in whether
the number would rise or fall above the
average thirty. This evening so many
feet passed his door, and there was such
a hum of life, that he concluded there
would be forty, which was a high attendance, and he began to reproach himself for cowardice and unbelief. He
was looking out the hymns when the
door opened, and Mr. Lovejoy came in
with such evident satisfaction upon his
gracious face that the minister was
certain some good thing had happened.
" Excuse me interrupting you," said

the good man, " but I came to ask whether you would mind going into the hall to-night? The room is full already, and more are coming every minute. I should not wonder to see a hundred, perhaps two," and Mr. Lovejoy beamed and quite unconsciously shook hands afresh with the minister.

" You may be sure that I shall be only too glad, but . . . what is the meaning of this? Do they know that I am preaching myself?" And the minister seemed anxious lest the people should have been brought in the hope of hearing some distinguished stranger.

" Of course, they know, and that is why they have come," responded Mr. Lovejoy with great glee; "no other person could have brought them, and if you didn't preach to-night, it would be the greatest disappointment the people ever had; but I must hurry off to see that everything is right in the hall," and in a minute the minister heard the

sound of many voices as the people
poured joyfully from the room into the
hall, and even in the vestry he was conscious of a congregation. As he was
speculating on the meaning of it all the
door opened again and Mr. Lovejoy
returned.

" We hadn't faith enough," he cried;
" we ought to have gone to the church
at once. Brother Stonier said in his
usual decided way, ' No half measures,
into the church with you;' but I was
afraid there would not be enough. I
was wrong, quite wrong, the church will
be nicely filled from back to front, for
the people are coming in a steady
stream—it's just great to see them. I'll
come back for you when they are all
seated; but give them time, it's not easy
moving from one place to another as
we've been doing to-night; but we'll not
move another Wednesday, we'll just
settle down in the church as in the

former days," and Mr. Lovejoy left the vestry walking on air.

When the minister went in the church was almost full, and he had some difficulty in giving out the first hymn, for it came upon him that his people had seen that he was discouraged and that this was a rally of affection. The prayer was even harder for him than the hymn, although his heart was deeply moved in gratitude to God and tender intercession for men. And then when he came to the address he threw aside what he had prepared, for it seemed to him too cold and formal, and he read the One Hundred and Twenty-sixth Psalm slowly and with a trembling voice, and instead of commentary, he paused between the verses, and the people understood. When he read the last verse—" He that goeth forth and weepeth, bearing precious seed, shall doubtless come again with rejoicing, bringing his sheaves with him "—he hesitated a moment, and then pronounced the benediction. After a minute's silent prayer he lifted his head and found the people still waiting. Mr. Judkin rose, and coming forward to the desk, thanked the minister audibly for all his work; and then they all came— men, women, and children—and each in his own way said the same thing; and the story went abroad that Richard Stonier, who came last and said nothing, had broken down for the first and only time in his life.

THE END.

Printed in the United States
20308LVS00002B/74